THE PROPERTY INVESTORS BLUEPRINT

A Black Belt Approach to Property Investing

DERVISH DERVISH

BLACK BELT INVESTOR

WOODBRIDGE
PUBLISHERS

Forest House, 3rd Floor 16-20
Clements Road Unit #2048
Ilford, IG1 1BA

978-1-80704-430-5 | (Paperback)
978-1-80704-432-9 | (Hardback)
978-1-80704-433-6 | (eBook)

Cover Design by Woodbridge Publishers.

Find out more about our upcoming releases and authors at www.woodbridgepublishers.co.uk and sign up for our newsletter to stay updated!

Dedication

To my three amazing children, may you grow with confidence, determination, and discipline. You have everything within you to achieve whatever you choose in life. Never stop growing into who you are capable of becoming.

Contents

Introduction;
Build Wealth, Not Just A Portfolio

When people ask me why I invest in property, the answer is simple: it builds wealth. Not through overnight miracles or flashy schemes, but steadily, predictably, and powerfully over time. I've experienced it firsthand. I bought my first buy-to-let in 2007. It was a modest property, nothing glamorous, and I made nearly every mistake a new investor can make: overpaying, failing to negotiate, hiring the cheapest trades, and skipping proper tenant checks. And yet, despite all that, it still made money.

More importantly, it taught me a crucial lesson: property works even when you don't get it perfect the first time. That principle has guided every investment I've made since. Over the years, I deliberately and intentionally grew my portfolio, focusing on resilience and sustainable growth rather than chasing quick wins. When my main business, a martial arts academy I had built over nearly two decades, took a significant hit during the pandemic, my property income continued uninterrupted. That steady, reliable cash flow is what financial resilience looks like, and it is what I want to help others achieve.

I'm not here to sell illusions. There is no magic formula, no "*£10k months from your first deal,*" and no shortcut to instant freedom. My approach is grounded in real-world experience, consistent execution, and structured guidance. Since 2007, I've completed many BRRRs, BTLs, and HMOs. I've navigated financing, renovations, tenant management, and market fluctuations. Through it all, I've built a profitable portfolio that supports my family and funds the life I want.

I also bring a different perspective through my background as a 6th Dan Black Belt and long-term martial arts school owner. I've coached thousands of students and guided hundreds to achieve their Black Belts. The philosophy, discipline, and mentorship that shaped those students are exactly what I now bring to property investing. Inside the **Black Belt Property Academy**, I guide investors from White Belt beginners to Black Belt professionals, providing structured mentorship, accountability, and the confidence to execute successfully.

This book is about helping you develop the mindset, strategy, and systems required to build a property portfolio that truly works. You'll learn how to identify and fund profitable deals, avoid costly mistakes, manage refurbishments efficiently, and operate strategically rather than reactively. The lessons I share are the same ones that underpin my mentoring programme, designed to take you further than you thought possible while developing the discipline and clarity to succeed independently.

Property investing isn't just about numbers; it's about consistent, informed action. It's about building a framework that works for you, not relying on luck or following generic advice. This book distills over fifteen years of hands-on experience, mentoring, and personal lessons into practical guidance, so you can start making confident, strategic decisions for your portfolio and your future.

Let's get started.

Dervish Dervish
Founder, Black Belt Property Academy
6th Degree Black Belt | Author | BSc | PGCE

PART 1

Property Foundations & Mindset

Before you dive into strategies and deals, you need a solid foundation. This section explores why property is one of the most powerful wealth-building tools, why timing matters, and how compounding can work in your favour. You'll also learn the mindset shifts that separate successful investors from the rest, and the key numbers you must understand to make smart, profitable decision.

Chapter 1

Why Invest In Property?

Property gives you the rare ability to earn a monthly income, benefit from long-term capital growth, and have your mortgage paid down by your tenant. It is one of the strongest ways to protect yourself from inflation while building generational wealth through an asset people will always need, a home.

What a great question to ask. I'm sure that since you are reading this book, you are either a property investor or seriously considering becoming one. You are likely to have your own reasons, but within this chapter are my thoughts and reasons for investing in property.

Property investing is one of the most effective strategies for building your wealth, securing your financial future, and generating long-term passive income.

When you start implementing the information in this book, you should start building wealth and achieving financial freedom. I'm not going to 'sell you the dream' and tell you it happens overnight because that would be a lie. It takes time, but it doesn't take a lifetime.

I've been a property investor since 2007, and although there are the bad times, headaches, and the 'why do I even bother' days, overall, it's a very good investment tool. I've listed some of the benefits below, but a quick answer to the 'why invest in property' question would be…

People always need somewhere to live – fact!

Here in the UK, property is in demand; the government isn't building enough houses and hasn't since the 1970s. With a growing population, that means there are more people needing houses than there are houses available. For property investors, it's economics lesson 101: supply and demand.

Everybody Needs Somewhere To Live

Having shelter is one of our basic survival needs. You therefore have a product that many people want to buy/rent. In the UK, it's in very short supply, and people need it now more than ever. In our investment area, there are still over 20 'good' applicants per rental property that we finish. We have a major housing shortage in the UK, so why not take run-down houses, turn them into nice accommodation, and earn some money from them? Doing so is a win-win situation; you are providing much-needed housing and earning from that service.

There are lots of things that attract me to property, and it's not that I like touching the bricks, running my hand along smooth plaster, or choosing which shower to install. I don't like deciding where new electrical points are going to go or what front door to choose. I do like when everything's done and it's ready to be let (or sold, we rarely sell because wealth is created by keeping hold of the assets). I definitely do not love either the refurbishment or even the conveyancing process. However, they are all part and parcel of the process, and there must be a reason that we haven't stopped investing since 2007. Some of the reasons are below.

Reasons Why We Invest In Property

- If purchased at the correct price, you have locked in profit from day 1
- Provides positive monthly cash flow (can be 99% passive)
- A higher return on capital employed (ROCE) than any bank can offer
- Its ability to be leveraged to invest in more property, which means more cash flow and more capital growth
- Over time, the asset grows in value whilst the debt remains fixed
- (somewhat) passive income
- The opportunity to create wealth for future generations
- You have input on how the property performs, unlike with stocks, shares, and bonds (though diversifying your assets is always a good practice)
- Property is tangible, unlike stocks, shares, and bonds
- You can leverage property, lenders won't lend you money to buy stocks and shares (or watches, crypto, etc.), but they will lend you money to buy property
- Over time, inflation reduces the amount of your mortgage loan
- Capital growth occurs if you hold the property for the long term, meaning your initial deposit/investment is worth far more down the line. You cannot predict when or how much capital growth will occur because it doesn't follow a linear path and depends on where we are in the property cycle (more about this later in the book)

- You can leverage other people's money (OPM) to your advantage (anybody who invests with a property developer should get better returns than banks are offering)
- You can achieve outstanding Return On Capital Employed (ROCE), and in some cases, you can have an infinite ROCE. I expand more on this in the BRRR section
- You can recycle your cash and move on to the next property for bigger returns
- There are many ways you can make a property work for you rather than just the traditional 'single let' model; you can multi-let it by the room, change it to serviced accommodation, and more. I expand on strategies later in the book

In Summary

There are many upsides to investing in property; you should benefit from an increase in wealth, an increase in cash flow, and your debt should erode over time. Yes, as with any business, there is a downside, but I believe the upside far outweighs the downside of property investing.

Chapter 2

Why You Need To Start Investing Now?

In property, delay costs more than mistakes, and missed opportunities don't show up on your balance sheet. The earlier you start, the more time you give your wealth to grow.

Although the benefits of property are widely known, many would-be investors and potential millionaires delay investing in property for several reasons: they are too busy, it's not the right time, what if there's a crash, what if I get a bad tenant, etc.

The thing is, though, that the earlier you start, the more time you have in the market, and the chances of your success do increase. For those who start early, the benefits can be profound. I wish that I'd started sooner.

If you decide to delay your investing, you miss out on 3 main things:

1. Property appreciation & the compounding law (covered later)
2. Rental Income & its growth year on year (this is passive income)
3. Reinvesting and portfolio expansion

The Right Time

So, if you are reading this now, thinking that you will just wait for Summer, Christmas, the kids to be a bit older, until you have more experience, until you have read another 5 books, or any of the other endless reasons. You are leaving money on the table. Imagine not buying a property this year and finding that same property has increased by £20k by next year. Or that in 5 years the property you could have bought for £100k is now worth £160k+, maybe even £200k.

I am not suggesting going out and buying anything, and I'm not saying to overpay, but we should remember it is time in the market, not timing the market.

The sooner you start, the sooner your education begins. By investing sooner rather than later, you position yourself to benefit from inflation, rather than falling victim to it. Some of the worst deals we've done are where we haven't bought the property. They don't show up on our PnL, but I know we missed out on by many 10's of £1'000's by not purchasing the property.

The longer you are in the market, the more deals you will see and the more you will benefit from securing these deals.

If you wait for all the traffic lights to turn green or for all the stars to align, you may miss out on life-changing opportunities. The perfect time does not exist. There is rarely ever the perfect time. Remember the saying, '*the best time to plant a tree was 20 years ago, the second best time is now*', the same is true in property. I wish we had bought more in those early years from 2007 to 2017. Imagine how much wealthier we would be, plus how much more passive income we would have collected.

In Summary

Starting your property investing journey asap will clearly benefit you. The law of compounding will have more time to work than delaying your start, meaning you won't build as much equity as you could have done if you had started earlier. To be successful in property, you need a willingness to learn, and the sooner you start, the sooner you start learning.

Chapter 3
Why Property Wins In The Long Game?

Markets wobble, tenants come and go, but over the long game, well-bought property almost always wins.

Stocks Vs Property: What's The Safer Bet?

When you invest in stocks or businesses and make a mistake, you can lose everything. Companies go bust, shares tank, and the value can literally hit zero. But with property, even if things go wrong, you usually just lose a bit, not everything. In 10 years, that property will have probably increased in value. I was in negative equity across my 3 properties during the financial crash of 2009, but bricks and mortar have a way of bouncing back. That's not always the case with the stock market.

Why Passive Income Beats Trading Time For Money?

One of the biggest reasons I love property is that your money works harder than it ever could sitting in a savings account (nobody ever became wealthy through saving alone). Once the property is up and running, you start earning passive income, with rent coming in every month, whether you're working or not. It's not 100% passive (let's be honest), but it's a damn sight easier than trading time for money every single day, especially if it's a job you hate.

Although it's a long time ago now, I remember the early days when the rents used to land in the account. It was a nice feeling realising that I didn't have to go and work for that money. Of course, we had the mortgage to pay, but that additional cash flow was a nice buffer. In the early days, I used to treat it as a little extra spending money since I had my salary from my lecturing job and my growing Karate school.

What Happens In A Crash?

At some point, the market will wobble again. There'll be another crash, or as it's properly called, a *market correction.* But like Warren Buffett says, *'Be fearful when others are greedy, and greedy when others are fearful."* That's how we operate, that's how our Black Belt investors operate. When prices do drop, it's like a '20–30% off' sale, that's when Black Belt investors buy more.

Property goes through cycles, yes, but if you zoom out to the last several hundred years, prices have always risen. Crash or no crash, if your property is still cash flowing each month, you don't need to panic or sell. You haven't lost anything unless you choose to sell at a loss.

Most people get it backwards. They buy high (when the market's hot) and panic sell low (when it drops). That's the opposite of what smart Black Belt investors do. Upon selling, you are crystallising your losses.

The Power Of Long-Term Thinking

There's a psychological trap called recency bias, where we think whatever's happening now is going to keep happening. But property isn't about what happens in the next 3 months. It's about what happens over 10+ years.

I believe in the buy-and-hold forever strategy. That's where real wealth is built, not in flipping, not in chasing the next shiny thing, but in staying in the market and letting time and compounding do the work.

Back in 2009, when the financial crash had plummeted property prices and I was in negative equity on all 3 I wanted to sell all of them. I was convinced I had made the worst mistake of my life. Who was I? The 26-year-old guy, thinking I was a property investor. I even put 1 up for sale for less than I had paid for it and still didn't sell it. In hindsight, though, keeping hold of those 3 properties was a great move. They have all doubled in price and, hopefully, will double again in the next 10-15 years.

Can You Lose Money In Property?

Of course, you can. You can lose money in any business venture. I've been in business for nearly 25 years, and my first was a single-location Martial Arts School I started in 2004. In most well-built businesses, you win 99% of the time and lose 1% and property's no different.

This is why due diligence is critical; you must know your numbers & know your market. Understand your own risk tolerance. Property carries risk, but in my view, it's a controlled risk. You get a say in the outcome. You can renovate, re-let, or refinance. You don't get that level of influence with shares or crypto.

Interest Rates: Accept The New Normal

Yes, interest rates have gone up, but we must keep some perspective.

Borrowing post-crash at 1–2% and for many years afterwards was an extremely good deal. Most people didn't know it, but that was a gift. My parents remember paying 12–13% back in the late 80s and early '90s, and I've heard stories of rates above 15% in the '70s. So if we're borrowing at 4–6% today, that's still manageable as long as the deal stacks.

You can't control interest rates, but you can control what deals you say yes to.

Ignore The Media Hype

"I heard there's going to be another crash!" Yes, there probably will be, there always is. But the media's job is to sell fear, not facts. Bad news gets more clicks. I don't watch or listen to any of it. Why would I fill my head with negativity when I could focus on improving my knowledge, helping my mentees, finding great deals, and building wealth?

When the next crash comes, we won't be hiding. We'll be investing in prime assets, smart deals, and income-generating properties. Even in a downturn, people still need somewhere to live. Rents still come in, and bills still get paid. Life goes on, and so does your portfolio.

Why Isn't Everyone Doing This?

Great question, why doesn't everyone invest in property if it's so good?

Well, why doesn't everyone eat healthy, exercise daily, and live a toxin-free life? We all know it's good for us, but that doesn't mean we do it. It takes effort and consistency. Not everyone wants that.

You, on the other hand, are reading this book. So I know you're thinking about your future and your goals. Property isn't easy, but there are much harder and riskier ways to build wealth.

The Ugly Bits (But We Still Love It)

It's not all sunshine and passive income. Here's what I don't like about property (and anyone being honest should admit the same):

- The moving tax goalposts
- Being gazumped
- The long, sometimes painful conveyancing process
- Financing falling through
- Refurbishments going over budget or time
- Contractors are letting you down
- Bridging finance running out
- Low valuations on refinance
- Bad tenants or tenants doing a runner owing you money
- More and more legislation and red tape

Still reading? Good, because while all of that can be frustrating, the rewards far outweigh the problems. As the old saying goes, 'the juice is worth the squeeze'.

One of the properties I first bought was a 2-bed end terrace. I had bad tenant after bad tenant. Looking back, though, it was 100% me, not the house. It was my fault for not vetting tenants properly and just thinking of the rent I was losing while it was empty. I wasn't building a business, though, and I definitely wasn't thinking long term; I was just looking to earn a bit of extra money. I always recommend you leave the property empty until you find a tenant who ticks all the boxes, rather than one you have a bad feeling about, just because you want the rent coming back in.

The Long Game Always Wins

If you're still sitting on the fence, let me remind you of this:

"Don't wait to buy property - buy property and wait."

We keep investing because property works. We buy assets that rise in value while the (good) debt gets eroded by inflation. We earn a monthly income and we build long-term wealth. We sleep at night knowing we've made smart decisions for our future.

Why Do You Want This?

Take a second and think:

- Do you want multiple holidays a year?
- Ample savings in your account?
- A car you're proud of?
- The freedom to work because you want to, not because you have to?
- True financial freedom?

Whatever your "*why*" is, property can be the vehicle that gets you there. You just need to take control and play the long game.

<u>In Summary</u>

Property isn't perfect, far from it, but it's one of the most resilient and forgiving investment vehicles out there. Unlike stocks or businesses that can go to zero, property tends to recover and grow over time, even after crashes. The key is thinking long-term, understanding the power of cash flow, and not panicking during market corrections. Yes, you'll face setbacks, from interest rate hikes to bad tenants, but if you buy well, manage smart, and stay in the game, property can deliver real wealth through passive income, capital growth, and inflation-eroded debt. It's not always easy, but the long game rewards those who commit. The choice is yours: stay on the fence, or get in the game and start building the life you want.

Chapter 4

Time + Property = Wealth
The Magic Of Compounding

Wealth isn't built overnight; it's built by letting time and smart decisions work together, quietly compounding your success while others chase shortcuts.

True wealth is created by understanding the law of compounding, and smart investors let time do the heavy lifting. Albert Einstein, who was a very clever man, described compounding as the 8th wonder of the world.

Compounding is when the returns on your investment start earning returns of their own, creating exponential growth over time. It can be described as your money earning money, and then that money earning even more money. It can be thought of as the snowball effect.

I tried to talk to my children about the power of compounding, and they understood the concept, but it wasn't until I got out an old monthly calendar that it started to sink in. I showed them that if you just have a 1p piece on day 1 and it doubles every day, by the time you get to the last day (day 30), that 1p is now worth over £10'000'000. Although our assets do not double every day (or even every year, though maybe every decade), it's a great way for them to understand the immense power of compounding.

Unfortunately, they don't teach '*compounding*' in school, so if you have children, make sure you teach them this important principle.

If we purchased a little 2-bed terrace property for £100k and we expect it to grow by a modest 5% each year, the following year it should have increased in value by 5% of £100k, which is £5k. In year 2, it will have grown 5% of the new £105k, not the original £100k, which would be £110'250. In year 3, it will have grown by 5% of the new amount, which would be £115'762, and so on. It would be wrong to assume, though, that in year 10 it would be 10 * 5% = 50% increase in the £100k and in year 20 it would be 20 * 5% = 100% increase. Have a look at the table below to see what compounding can do over 20 years.

<table>
<tr><th>Year</th><th>Value</th><th>5 % growth</th><th>New value</th></tr>
<tr><td>Day 1</td><td>£100’000</td><td>£5’000</td><td>£105’000</td></tr>
<tr><td>1</td><td>£105’000</td><td>£5’250</td><td>£110’250</td></tr>
<tr><td>2</td><td>£110’250</td><td>£5’513</td><td>£115’763</td></tr>
<tr><td>3</td><td>£115’763</td><td>£5’788</td><td>£121’551</td></tr>
<tr><td>4</td><td>£121’551</td><td>£6’078</td><td>£127’628</td></tr>
<tr><td>5</td><td>£127’628</td><td>£6’381</td><td>£134’010</td></tr>
<tr><td colspan="4">It’s grown £34k in 5 years</td></tr>
<tr><td>10</td><td>£162’889</td><td>£8’144</td><td>£171’034</td></tr>
<tr><td colspan="4">It’s grown £71k in 10 years
(£37k in last 5-year period)</td></tr>
<tr><td>15</td><td>£207’893</td><td>£10’395</td><td>£218’287</td></tr>
<tr><td colspan="4">It’s grown £118k in 15 years
(£47k in last 5-year period)</td></tr>
<tr><td>20</td><td>£265’330</td><td>£13’268</td><td>£278’596</td></tr>
<tr><td colspan="4">It’s grown £178k in 20 years
(£60k in last 5-year period)
The last 10 years it has grown over £100k</td></tr>
</table>

At first, it doesn’t seem to be growing that quickly. However, considering house prices in the UK have grown on average by 6% annually in recent years and by 74% over the last 20 years (according to Gov.uk), you can see how this impacts thing. We are great believers in ‘*buy and hold forever*’ because we know that real wealth creation comes from holding the asset. Yes, flips are great and, when done properly, generate large lumps of cash, but you only get the payout once. Every day you hold a property, you let compounding do its work.

Yes, there are property crashes and fluctuations, but in the long run, property has always gone up in value. You will notice that, over each 5 years, growth is larger than in the previous one. So, for shorter periods of time, the value increases far greater than it did in the earlier stages of holding the asset.

Now imagine having a nice portfolio of 10 or more properties, each growing like this. It is possible and is achievable, think bigger, think like a Black Belt investor, why not 15-20 properties, 100 properties. Build on that knowledge and then implement.

To really let the law of compounding have an effect, you need to hold the asset for the long term. The same is true for business. When I first started my Karate school back in January 2004, I really didn't know why I stayed open for the first few years. It hardly seemed worth it. I was a 2nd-degree Black Belt, but being skilled in Karate does not mean you are skilled in building and running a business. However, I knew that if I stuck with it, didn't jump into something else, and learned from people who had done what I wanted to do, then it would work out well, which it did. If you invest in a copy of the book, How to Build a Highly Profitable Martial Arts School, I'm sure it will help. You need to invest time in the success of your property journey.

In Summary

To be a successful investor, you need to understand the power of compounding. You can make nice lumps of cash flipping properties, but unless you reinvest that money back into assets you own, you will never create real wealth. Wealth is created by holding onto properties.

Chapter 5

Time Is Your Greatest Asset Use It Wisely

Money comes and goes, but time only goes. The fastest way to build wealth is to treat every minute as if it mattered.

Time is the most valuable asset we have. Unlike money, we cannot earn back once time has gone; that's it, it can never be reclaimed.

We all have 1440 minutes in a day, and no matter how hard we try, we can't extend the amount of time in a day, week, or month. We can, however, learn how to be more productive with our time so that we can achieve more. I strongly suggest you focus your attention so that you achieve your goals. This is not the time to write about time management strategies (there are 100's of books on the subject, and I believe a video or 2 on my YouTube channel). Still, I want to get across to you, the reader, that if you want to grow a property portfolio or indeed any business, and generate passive income, you must understand when you are being productive and not being productive. Don't be one of those people who constantly say, *'I don't know where time has gone.'* You need to know if you are wasting your time or using it wisely. The most successful people use their time wisely because they realise how valuable it is. They understand the 80/20 principle and that their profits come from 20% of what they do; they continually expand on that 20% to make their time as efficient as possible.

Spend Time To Get Money

Poor people spend time getting money, whereas wealthy people spend money to get time. If you can adopt this mindset shift, you are already on the right path. I know that sometimes it's much easier and quicker for you to do certain tasks because you can do it better than anybody else, but you must ask yourself, '*Is this the best use of my time?*'. At the start, you are probably the only person in your business, so you feel you need to do everything; however, as you progress, you need to become more resourceful.

Always ask '*who can do this*' rather than '*how can I do this*'. When you are trying to secure bridging finance or a mortgage, you employ a reputable broker. When you are purchasing a property, you don't think about doing the conveyancing work yourself; you employ trained professionals. When you pick up the keys to your property, you must run everything through the '*is this the best use of my time*' filter. I remember ripping out kitchens, scraping wallpaper off, crowbarring skirting boards, plus other things I shouldn't have been doing. I would charge +£100 for a private 1:1 karate lesson, yet go and do these £10-£15ph jobs. It was stupid; it was such a false economy. I could have done 2 * 60-minute private lessons and paid somebody to do all the other low-value jobs I used to get sucked into doing. I did it though because I wanted the refurb to keep moving or the property to be ready for re-let asap. So, if you have a well-paid job now or have your own company, then compare your normal hourly rate to what you would pay somebody to do the low-value tasks you can easily get dragged into. You are not getting into property to build another job; it's about building passive income and wealth.

I Haven't Got Time To Do This

When I hear my mentees say '*I haven't got time to do it.... I haven't got time for mentorship*,'' I shout back at them – that's exactly why you need to do it. If your days are so full that you cannot allocate time to build your passive income and wealth, then you need to step back and see where most of your time is being sucked up. From experience, 80% of what people do is not the best leverage of their time. I still fall into the trap now, but I'm a lot more aware of when it happens and then quickly pivot to something more effective that will take us where we need to go.

Zero Revenue Tasks

Think of all the tasks you currently do that bring in zero money: cleaning, cooking, washing the car, hoovering, gardening, etc. Now, of course, these are essential parts of living, but do you think wealthy people do these tasks? Before you say, '*Well, they are wealthy, they can afford to pay people*,' there's more to it than that. They realise that every minute they are not investing their time to bring back the biggest return, they are doing themselves a disservice. We all have to start somewhere, so maybe employ a cleaner for just 2 hours a week, then during those 2 hours, complete some high-value tasks that generate far more than the amount you pay the cleaner. If you pay a cleaner £20ph, totalling £40, but you earn £100 or even more, then that's a fantastic trade. Even if you earn £50 in that time frame, it's still a better use of your time. Trust me, I get it. This was very hard for me and my family because I felt I should be doing those things, but our business now runs much smoothly because we have bought back some time. We don't have a team waiting on us hand and foot for 24 hours a day, far from it, but taking off these 'zero revenue building tasks' has massively helped. I think it links back to the principle '*don't step over pounds to pick up pennies.* Imagine not being able to view a property that you could have made +£20-£50k on because you were busy doing zero-revenue tasks.

Do Things That Shift The Needle The Most

As a property investor, you should be doing things every day that move the needle the most in your business and life. For property investors at the start, that is research, viewings, offers, raising finance, and building relationships. As you become more established, you are likely to employ somebody or have a small team who will do the research, viewings, and offers. This then extends out to a project manager who is in charge of the refurbishments. One of the last tasks you should outsource is networking and raising finance.

When you invest time at the start of your property purchase to do a thorough refurbishment, then this will continue to pay you moving forward, i.e., you have invested your time. When I used to do weekly team training and more detailed, intense weekend team training, it was time invested because what I was teaching my team would improve my business moving forward.

Flicking through a magazine and watching hours of reality TV does not move you forward. Reading a book, attending a seminar, and joining a mastermind are time well invested because the skills you learn should help you move forward. It's up to you to strike the correct balance; nobody can work every minute they are awake without eventually burning out, but if you focus on the high-value tasks, you will grow.

In Summary

Our time is finite. We can earn more money, but we can never get back time. Start to think about the most productive 20% of your time, and expand those tasks, and you will become more successful.

Chapter 6

The Investor Mindset Most People Never Develop

The people who win in property aren't the smartest; they're the ones who start, continually educate themselves, stay consistent, and refuse to quit.

The Harsh Truth Most Won't Tell You

Most people who read books like this will never buy a single property. That might sound harsh, but it's the truth. They'll highlight the pages, nod along, and say, "*Yeah, I already know that…*"

But the real question is - are you actually doing it?

There's a big gap between knowing and doing. If you just take action on 10% of what's in this book, you'll already be ahead of 90% of people. You don't need to know it all; you just need to start.

Mindset Vs Skillset

Success in property doesn't go to the smartest person in the room or the one with the best contacts. It goes to the most consistent, the one who keeps getting up and showing up, the one with that Black Belt perseverance.

You can either make money or you can make excuses, but you can't make both. We all have that little voice that says, "*I'm no good at that.*" But remember this: the easiest person to lie to is yourself. Next time you catch yourself thinking *"I can't do that,"* just add one word: *"yet."*

"I can't do that... yet." That word changes everything.

Visualisation & Language: They Matter More Than You Think

Your words shape your reality. What you speak becomes what you believe, and what you believe becomes what you do. Start seeing yourself holding the keys to your first deal. Picture the rent coming in. The family home you've always dreamed of.

Write your goals down. Read them out loud every day. Make it real in your mind before it becomes real in your life. When you repeat that vision to yourself every day, your brain starts believing it's not only possible, it's inevitable. I'm not a fan of manifestation, probably because I haven't applied it; however, I do believe in having a positive mental attitude and having clearly defined goals.

Commitment Over Time Beats Talent Every Time

You can take the exact same steps as someone else and not get the same results at first.

But most people quit just before it gets good. One of my mentees did more deals in 2023 than he did in the entire 5 years before that. But none of that would've happened if he hadn't started back in 2013.

Momentum takes time to build, but once it's moving, it becomes unstoppable. Yes, property is hard, but you know what's harder? Staying in a job you hate for 40 years and then relying on an overly stretched government to look after you during retirement.

Confidence, Rejection, & Resilience

Rejection is part of the game. Some agents won't take you seriously at first, and that's fine. You only need one agent who will. Once you get those first few deals over the line, those same people will suddenly want to know you.

You will get knock-backs, people will doubt you, and you'll make mistakes. None of that is a reason to stop. If you want to do something great, you have to get uncomfortable. That's where growth happens, outside the comfort zone.

Belief Comes First

If even one person has done it, you can too. The only difference is that they started and they kept going. Stop playing and thinking small. Start saying things out loud like:

- *"This year I'm buying my first investment property."*
- *"This year I'm adding £1,000/month in passive income."*
- *"This year I'm going to learn how to build a profitable property portfolio."*

Tell people you trust what you want to do. If you feel confident to do so, then make bold declarations. Why? Because it holds you accountable, and it starts shifting your identity. When you start believing you're the type of person who takes action, you become that person.

The Window Is Closing

Every day you wait, the window to change your life gets smaller. There's no perfect time. You'll never have every answer, and you can't wait for all the traffic lights to turn green. But the people who win are the ones who move, learn, adjust, and keep going.

In Summary

Success in property is rarely about knowing more; it's about doing more. Your mindset, consistency, and ability to take bold action will determine how far you go. The people who win in this game aren't the ones with the fanciest spreadsheets; they're the ones who stay focused, bounce back from rejection, and show up even when it's hard. If you take even 10% of this seriously and actually apply it, you'll outperform 90% of people who never get off the starting blocks. Start building on that Black Belt mindset, and the results will follow.

Chapter 7

Key Metrics: The Numbers That Make Or Break A Deal

Amateurs guess, but professionals know the numbers. Get the numbers right, and you'll move fast, negotiate hard, and invest with confidence.

Before you ever walk through the door of a property, the numbers should already be telling you a story.

Whether it's the cash flow, return on capital, or refinance potential, these metrics are what separate aspiring investors from serious wealth builders. Get them wrong, and you risk losing time, money, and momentum. Get them right, and you'll have the confidence to move quickly, negotiate hard, and build a portfolio that truly pays you now and in the long term.

In this chapter, I'll walk you through the key property metrics I focus on when analysing new deals and tracking the profitability of existing properties in my portfolio. These include:

- Monthly Cash Flow
- Gross and Net Yield
- Return On Investment (ROI)

- Return On Capital Employed (ROCE)
- Capital Growth
- Capitalisation Rate
- How to calculate the interest payable on the loan
- How to calculate possible refinance values

Once you understand these numbers and how they work together, you'll be able to assess deals with clarity and confidence, avoid common mistakes, and make better buying decisions, every time.

Monthly Cash Flow

For most investors at all stages of their investing journey, this is a good metric to assess. Cash flow is the money you are left with each month after your fixed expenses have been paid. I say fixed expenses because that is the best cash flow you will ever have from that property.

Example 1

Rent = £750 pcm
- Mortgage = £400 pcm
- Building insurance = £20 pcm
Cash flow = £330 pcm

If a managing agent manages the property, then your fixed expenses would increase, for example:

Rent = £750 pcm
- Mortgage = £400 pcm
- Building insurance = £20 pcm
- 10% (+ vat) of the rent = £90
Cash flow =£240 pcm

You may choose to manage it yourself. If you do, then make sure you pay yourself the 10% you would pay a managing agent. Nobody else would work in your business for free, so why should you? I am not a financial advisor, so I cannot speak to you about your account about how to do this properly.

What About Other Expenses?

The highest your cash flow will be is the money you are left with when only the fixed expenses have been taken into account. The cash flow will reduce with any type of expense.

- Annual gas safety certificate (approx. £80)
- Property maintenance: anything that needs fixing, leaky tap, broken window handle, flickering lights, all the way to a new roof and full damp works
- Void periods
- Tenancy set-up fees: marketing, setting up the AST, and inventory (approx. £250-£600)

Our Minimum Cash Flow

Of course, each deal is analysed on its own merits, but we want a minimum of £300pcm per single BTL property. Some of our best single lets are £450-£515pcm, which may or may not seem a lot to you, but it's good to remember that money that drops into the account every month is 99% passive. For 4-6 bed HMO, we want a minimum of £1000 cash flow per property.

Negative Cash Flow

We have never invested in a property if it is cash flow negative each month. You may find it strange that I would need to write that down, but some investors are willing to take a short-term hit with cash flow (because it's not needed for them as much) for the long-term gain in capital value.

Rent 2 Rent & Cash Flow

If you want to apply the rent-to-rent model, discussed later in this book, then cash flow is the most important metric you have. You need to make sure that the money you make on the property minus what you have arranged to pay the landlord/vendor is as high as possible.

Cash flow is the money you are left with each month, and it can vary. Your job is to make the cash flow as high as possible and to build on it year on year.

Gross & Net Yield

When you start to speak to estate agents, they tend to speak a lot about 'yield'. Now, yield is a baseline measure. It gives you the absolute broad strokes of a deal and lets you know if it's worthy of taking it a step further. It is an easy and simple way to compare properties. A good understanding of yields allows you to decide if the property should be pursued further. When agents speak of 'yield,' what they are referring to is 'gross' yield.

Gross Yield

Yield is best described as the ratio of rental income to purchase price.

Example

If the property is £100'000 and it has a rent of £750pcm, then the yield would be calculated like so:

Total rent per year = £750 pcm × 12 = £9,000 pa
Gross yield = Annual rent /purchase price
9% = £9,000 / £100,000

The figure above is the gross yield, and as you can see, it is very easy to calculate. This is often the figure that gets thrown around by agents because it makes the deal look better than it is. The purchase price above does not take into consideration other fees such as the SDLT, legals, search, broker, and survey fees, all of which are discussed later. The purchase price would therefore be more like £108k approx. (At the time of writing, the SDLT in the UK is 5% of PP for investors.) As investors wanting to get the best return possible, we need to be concerned with the net yield because that's a more accurate figure, but it is also heavily dependent on our own circumstances.

Gross yield, though, should be thought of as a benchmark in which to compare properties.

Net Yield

Net yield is how much you are left with after your fixed expenses have been paid, i.e., mortgage/finance costs, building insurance, managing fees, service charges, etc. So, let's look at the same property again, but with some fixed expenses built into the equation.

Total Rent pa = £750pcm * 12 = £9000 pa

Net Yield	= cash flow pa/purchase price
Cash flow	= rent – fixed expenses
	= rent @£750pcm
	– mortgage £400pcm
	– building insurance £20pcm
	– management fee 10% + vat of rent = £90pcm
	= £240pcm
Net Yield	= cash flow pa/purchase price
	= £240 *12 / £100'000
	=£2'880 / £100'000
	= 2.8%

The basic examples above show that gross yield is a good metric to look at, but net yield is the more important one. Don't get too disheartened yet, though; there are more important metrics to look at than net yield.

It's very hard for a deal sourcer or agent to refer to the net yield because it depends on other variables that the agent is not likely to know. For example, if you are buying the property with a mortgage or cash, if it's a mortgage, then what's the rate, etc? What maintenance must be done?

The net yield will always vary, though from year to year, dependent on the maintenance needed and void periods. For example, 1 of our properties needed a new roof and a new boiler in the same year; there was no cash flow for that property for that year and well into the next. Cash flow is a good reason to invest in property, but the main reasons for us are to make our money work harder for us than in the bank and to benefit from the capital growth.

Some hands-off investors may not be bothered about the yields because they might be looking just to lock away some of their money since they know their money is better in the property than it would be sitting in the bank, earning far less. You need to decide your '*why*' for investing, and if the deal meets that, then go for it. Never just invest because somebody with zero property investing experience says, *'it's a good deal'*. Black Belt investors listen to more experienced people, those who are further on the journey than they are.

2.8% - I'm Better Off Leaving Money In The Bank

When I speak to new property investors, it's understandable that they think that it's not worth it for a 2.8% return. Back in 2007-2008, I would have agreed with them; however, the net yield is based on the full purchase price. It's unusual for investors not to leverage their money by only putting down 25% as a deposit and raising the rest through a mortgage, JV partner, or a straight loan from an investor. When you look at it through those eyes, the yield becomes much better; this is where ROCE comes in. ROCE is a metric we look at when analysing deals (more on this later).

What Is A Good Yield?

Again, this depends on your investment strategy and area. As an investor, you need to decide the criteria for a deal. This is likely to evolve over time as your wealth and cash flow increase, but during your first few deals, you need to know your benchmarks.

You may decide that you want a net yield of at least 7% or higher, it all depends on why you are investing in property, is it to get you out of a job you hate, is it because you have a successful business and want to use the profits from that to invest, or is it because you want to become a successful property investor and have great amounts of passive income each and every month.

In some investment areas, the cash flow is not great, so your yield will be bad, but the capital growth will far outpace average norms (London has terrible yields but great capital growth). For investors not too fussed about the monthly cash flow, they can sit back and watch the asset grow year on year and then sell or refinance when they want. They know that money invested in that property has a far greater return than sitting in any bank.

In our investment area, we work with a minimum of an 8% yield but a return on capital employed of at least 30%.

I urge you to stick to those benchmarks and not get caught up in something because the agent said, *'it's a great deal'*. The deals you choose to invest time and money into should meet your specific investment goals.

Potential Expenses

During your investment journey, you are likely to incur some or all of the following expenses:

- Bridging finance payments
- Mortgage payments
- Building insurance
- Management letting fees
- Maintenance costs
- Void periods
- Cosmetic work in between tenancies
- Marketing and set-up fees for sourcing a new tenant

- Holding fees for utility companies, etc
- Annual gas safety and fire safety checks

The more experienced you become, the better you will be at it, i.e., you will be able to speed up any refurbishments, secure a qualified tenant sooner, etc.

Return On Investment (ROI)

Return on Investment (ROI) is one of the most widely used metrics in property investing because it tells you how hard your money is working. It shows, as a percentage, how much profit you're making compared to how much you've invested. For example, if you invest £25,000 into a deal (including deposit, fees, refurb, etc.) and it gives you £2,500 profit per year, your ROI is 10%. That means for every £1'000 you put in, you're earning £100 annually.

While ROI helps compare one deal to another, it doesn't give you the full picture on things like refinancing potential or long-term wealth. That's why it's important to view ROI alongside other metrics like Return on Capital Employed (ROCE) and cash flow. But as a starting point, understanding your ROI helps you quickly assess whether a deal meets your minimum investment criteria and whether it's worth pursuing.

When calculating the Return On Investment (ROI), you can also include the capital growth because, in theory, the asset has increased, so your investment has grown. Just be aware, though, of making the deal sound better than it really is; never fudge the numbers.

Any investor who wants to make their money work harder needs to know the basics of gross and net yield. They allow you to decide if a deal is worth going for or passing on. The further you travel along your Black Belt property journey, the more granular you will become with the numbers.

Return On Capital Employed (ROCE)

Out of all the metrics that you can track with property investing, this is the one that we really base a deal on. Cash flow is great, especially when it's passive, but the ROCE is our number 1 metric. ROCE stands for

Return
On
Capital
Employed

In its simplest form, ROCE is the % return you expect based on the actual money you have in the deal. Here are a couple of examples to demonstrate how to calculate ROCE:

Example 1:

If we have £20'000 left in a deal and the property cash flows £250pcm, then our ROCE is calculated like so:

£250 pcm × 12 months = £3000 pa
£3000 ÷ £20,000 = 0.15

ROCE = 15%

Example 2:

See how the ROCE differs when we have more money in the deal and less cash flow. If we have £30'000 left in a deal and the property cash flows £200pcm, then our ROCE is calculated like so:

£200 × 12 months = £2400
£2400 ÷ £30,000 = 0.08

ROCE = 8%

From the 2 examples above, you can see how leaving more money in a deal and earning less cash flow reduces the ROCE. In the grand scheme of things, the cash flow is only £50 less pcm, and there is an extra £10k left in the deal, but the ROCE nearly halves. This is another reason that if you are implementing the BRRR strategy, you need to make sure the deal stacks in 3 scenarios: low valuation, market valuation, and high valuation.

It's your job as a savvy Black Belt property investor to get the ROCE as high as possible. I know many investors who have made the elusive infinite return on ROCE because they are managing to pull all their money out of the deal when using the BRRR strategy. To do this, you need to buy at a really low price and add a great deal of value way above the cost of the refurb. Leaving zero money means that you own an asset that is providing you with cash flow every month and the promise of capital growth without having any money left in the deal.

What Is A Good ROCE?

This is entirely dependent on your investment objectives. A good question I ask my mentees is *'how does your* ROCE *compare to what current interest rates are in the bank'*. This is always a good question to ask yourself when you look back on earlier deals you have done. If the ROCE is not as high as you like, remember that you are still 'in' the market and it's still earning better returns than a savings account.

For us, we need to have a minimum of a 20% ROCE. This is harder to achieve currently with single BTLs since the market is still on that upward trend, but it is much more achievable with HMOs.

How Can You Manipulate The ROCE?

- Your purchase price, the lower you pay for the property, the more you have locked in profit from the day you pick up the keys. This is 1 of the key elements I help my mentees master; they must lock in profit from day 1 because it has a huge impact on their overall investing success
- Your refurb cost
- The interest you have to pay on borrowed money

Will Your ROCE Remain The Same?

No! The above examples are based on cash flow, which means the money left over after your mortgage has been paid and your building insurance has been taken out.

What About When You Spend Money On Maintenance?

If you need to fit a new roof at a cost of £6'000 and your cash flow for the year doesn't equal that amount (£500pcm), then obviously your ROCE is reduced. I believe there needs to be a cut-off point because, at the end of the day, it's an investment, and there will always be money that needs to be spent, void periods, and an increase/decrease in borrowing costs. You could even build in the fact that you need a new carpet every 5 years, so that eats away at your ROCE. For our portfolio with our back-to-brick refurbs, if we know we have made the house like new, then we are future-proofing it somewhat, which should preserve our ROCE.

In summary, the higher you can make your ROCE, the better an investment it is. You will find that the more experienced and the more educated you become, the better your ROCE is.

Capital Growth

Capital growth is great because it just ticks along with time. If you have an annual capital growth of 4% per year, then with a £100k house, it's growing £4k each year (well, more really if you look at the compounding). So, when you are looking at your yields, you could also consider the capital growth in your calculations, too. Just be wary, though, that you can't spend capital growth or equity unless you refinance. Capital growth does not grow in a linear fashion either; there's that 80/20 principle in action again. We discuss this more in the property cycle chapter later.

One of our properties cash flows £285pcm but has grown £70k in 15 years. There are better performing numbers, but the fact that we completed on this about 2 months before the financial crash of 2008 just goes to show that the market does pick up again. £70k may or may not sound like a lot of money, but that's an increase of 120%. We earned approximately £4.6k per annum for simply owning the property. If your strategy is 'hold forever' and you start to build up a portfolio, you will greatly feel the benefits of all those £4k little money boxes grow each year. Imagine having a portfolio of £1'000'000 and gaining £40k growth in just 1 year for simply holding the property – not too shabby at all.

Capitalisation Rate

From speaking to many investors, including many mentors I have had over the years, 'cap rate' is not something that is commonly tracked. I feel it is useful for property investors to be aware of it and know what it means. I've always thought of it as similar to net yield.

To calculate the Cap Rate;

Cap Rate = Net operating profit/purchase price

The only difference between net yield and cap rate is your mortgage/finance costs (all other expenses are included). Cap rate is useful because it indicates the profitability of the property. Net yield can vary widely because each investor is likely to pay differing amounts for finance. When you calculate the cap rate, it doesn't take into consideration finance, so it gives the investor the amounts they would expect.

How To Work Out The Loan Amount, i.e, The Mortgage/Bridging?

Multiply the property price by 0.75 (the maximum loan for BTL is 75%, although some lenders allow you to go to 80%.

Example

Property price × 0.75
£100,000 × 0.75 = £75,000
The loan amount = £75k

How To Work Out The Interest Payments?

The following is based on a 5.5% interest rate. Please exchange the 0.055 for the rate you will hopefully achieve at the time of receiving your mortgage offer.

Multiply the loan amount by 0.055 (5.5% interest)

Example

loan amount * 0.055

=£75'000 * 0.055 = £4'125

This is the annual interest that needs to be paid to calculate the monthly payment, then divide the above by 12

= £4'125 / 12 = £343.75

This is the monthly interest that needs to be paid

nb. The interest % could be higher, so keep up to date with interest %'s, don't underestimate the %, always be at least 0.5% above, ideally 1% above. Or this may be easier for you to calculate:

Example

To work out the annual mortgage on £75,000
Find 1 percent of the mortgage debt £75,000 ÷ 100 = £750
Multiply that by the mortgage rate (5.5 percent) £750 × 5.5 = £4125

This gives the annual mortgage interest =£4125
Divide by 12 for the monthly amount **£4125 ÷ 12 = £343.75**

How To Calculate Possible Refinance Values?

To do this, we need to look at comparable properties in the area, i.e., a 2-bed terrace that has just had a good refurb should be compared to the exact same property type. A 3-bed semi cannot be compared to a 3-bed apartment, etc.

After looking at 3 comparable properties and working out the average across all 3, we should have a good idea of the value of the property. 1 property OTM for £120k, another for £125k, another for £130k. This would mean the average is £125k

From this average amount, we should then work out the loan-to-value (LTV). To do this, multiply the average by 0.75%

£125,000 × 0.75 = **£93,750**

From that, we then work out how much money we would be able to pull out by taking away the original loan from the new loan amount, plus any money on holding costs and refurbishment

£93,750 – £75,000 (original loan) – £10,000 (refurb and holding)
= £8,750
This is the amount pulled back out = **£8,750**

In Summary

Numbers are the foundation of every great property deal. By understanding and applying key metrics like cash flow, yield, ROI, and ROCE, you'll be able to analyse deals quickly and confidently. Always aim to lock in profit from day one by buying below market value, using realistic assumptions, and remember that quality refurbishments can push end values beyond local comparables. When you master the numbers, you stop guessing and start investing like a professional.

PART 2

Becoming A Professional Investor

This section is all about levelling up. You'll learn the key differences between amateurs and professionals, how to think long-term, and what mindset is needed to stay in the game. We'll cover why most investors fail, how to avoid their mistakes, and essential concepts like the property cycle, business structures, and industry terminology that every serious investor must understand.

Chapter 8

Why Most Investors Fail And How You Won't?

The difference between failure and success in investing isn't just strategy, it's mindset. Believe you deserve wealth, commit to constant learning, and act decisively. Waiting for perfect knowledge is the enemy of progress. Surround yourself with winners, invest in your education, and implement relentlessly. This mindset will set you apart.

This is how you avoid failing....Get educated & implement, that's it.

I stumbled into property investing in 2007. My dad encouraged me to buy a house. If you were around at that time, you will remember that everywhere you looked, there were adverts for property investing, seminars were taking place in hotels, there were buy-Spanish-holiday-home conventions, people were talking about it in the pub, plus much more. When people who have never invested before start giving advice, it's a bad situation.

One thing we teach mentees is that you can't expect to learn everything before you start. Yes, read 1-2 books and attend a seminar, but don't try to get all your ducks in a row. It's absurd to think you can know everything about a subject before leaping. It's crazy to think, but I read 0 books, went to 0 seminars, bought 3 properties just before the 2008 financial crash, and still made money in property. I am not saying that to brag, I'm saying it so you understand the importance of action. Our portfolio, cash flow, and wealth substantially increased as soon as I started educating myself. I'm reminded of Jim Rohn's famous quote, *"Formal education will make you a living, but self-education will make you a fortune."* When all is said and done, you just need to jump in because you will never be 100% ready. There are just too many variables that you can't control.

Over the years, I have attended numerous 1-day property events, several 3–4-day intensive courses, and enroled in 2 * 12-month property mentor programmes. I have probably read about 40 property books and listened to about 30 audio books. Before I started mentoring fellow property investors, I had a portfolio of +10 properties and had been formally educating myself for 4 years and informally through books and magazines for much longer. Do I regret it? No, but if I could go back, I would start to educate myself sooner. I'm a firm believer that you need to keep learning if you want to keep improving, but you need to keep implementing what you learn. Knowledge is only half the battle; implementation is what really matters.

I'm a mindset man and believe that our mindset has a huge impact on our lives and success. We need to believe we deserve to be wealthy and successful genuinely. Have an abundance mindset and appreciate that money needs to flow, but it flows into income-producing assets, not liabilities (liabilities are ok if you have lots of income-producing assets paying for them).

Here in the UK, we have a poppy-cutter culture, and success or wealth is not celebrated, you need to ensure you are surrounded by positive people who want you to succeed. Mentees in the **Black Belt Property Academy** want each other to succeed.

What Are Your Beliefs About Money: Are They Positive or Negative?

Have you ever said any of these?

- I attract money
- I have knowledge that when applied, it increased my income and wealth
- Money is not bad, it's a tool that I can use to improve my life

Carrying more money around in your wallet or purse is a nice feeling, it can prevent you from feeling like you have no money. Give yourself permission to carry around more than £10-£20. Yes, you have debit and credit cards, but having tangible money in your pocket is a nice feeling (well, it is to me).

Don't worry about finding an amazing deal; they are out there, you just need to look for them. You will find that the deal of the decade comes around once every few weeks if you know what you are looking for, like everything, where focus goes, energy flows. So, if you focus on finding properties, you will find some diamonds in the rough.

You must build your millionaire mindset, after all, success is 20% strategy and 80% mindset.

In summary, your mindset will have a huge impact on your success, as will your beliefs about money and your deserving it. I have a kaizen mindset and so want to improve continually, so yes, keep educating yourself and keep improving, but make sure you pull the trigger, don't wait to get all your ducks in a row.

Education: Do You Need To Go On Expensive Courses And Masterminds?

Now, of course, I have an interest in saying yes, you do, since I offer unique mentoring to driven and committed property investors; however, the choice is 100% yours. You will pay in 1 way or another, through time and mistakes or through education. I know from experience that I left £100,000s on the table because, for the first few years, I didn't seek any help. Education speeds up your success rate.

You may have read my other book, 'How to Build a Highly Profitable Martial Arts School?' in which I explain how I managed to grow my business to a very good level compared to anybody in my town.

After starting my Karate school in 2004, I was taking approximately. £8-£10k pcm in 2010, which is far better than industry norms (they were doing £1-£3k pcm). This left me with about £4-5k in monthly profit (not too shabby for a 27-year-old). I had pondered over investing in mentors for years, but the truth of the matter was '*I didn't know what I didn't know.*' In my eyes, I was doing very well, had no debt, drove a nice car, lived in a nice house, had savings, went on holidays, etc.

Looking back, though, I was just trading time for money; it was 100% earned income and 0% passive. Now, I knew about a mentor in America who was helping martial arts school owners gross over £100kpcm, which was 10X what I was doing. I was very sceptical, as I'm sure you may be, about all the property trainers out there.

However, after sitting on the fence for way too long, I jumped in. To cut a long story short, my school doubled in profits within 12 months, and I hated leaving it for so long. My school started to gross £30-£35kpcm every month. Here is the thing, though, I was not 100% fully implementing what they told me to - I was spreading myself too thin and trying to build up the property side of our income at the same time. I could have easily built it to +£50kpcm if I had been 100% focused.

Investing in a mentor speeds up your journey and helps you avoid costly mistakes that waste time and money. The investment you make in a mentor should yield a fantastic ROI if you implement their advice and listen to their guidance. I know that when I first started investing back in 2007, if I had had a mentor, I would have made much quicker progress and be much, much wealthier than I am today.

In Summary

The investment in a mentorship should be seen as exactly that, an investment and not just another expense. Trying to do it all alone is hard and slow (I know I did it for years). A mentor with a well-designed programme that doesn't just provide you with information, but who cares about your growth, will help you raise your game, which in turn should help grow your portfolio, cash flow, and wealth.

Chapter 9

What Separates Amateurs From Professional Investors?

Success isn't about knowing everything; it's about mindset, action, and resilience. Commit fully, start now, and surround yourself with winners.

Most people who pick up a book like this will never do a single deal. It's harsh but true.

Why? Because they want results without committing to the identity. If you want to be successful in any endeavour, you need to commit.

If you implement even 10% of the strategies in this book, you'll outperform 90% of the people who read it. Imagine your results if you fully committed to the journey. You don't need to know it all; you just need to do something. You just need to start and get better as you go.

Success in property doesn't start with spreadsheets. It starts with your mindset.

Mindset Over Skillset

It took me 10 years in business to realise that success doesn't go to the most educated or the most connected. It goes to the most committed and consistent. It goes to those who keep getting up and showing up, those who develop what I call '*Black Belt Determination.*'

As I mentioned in an earlier chapter, you can make money, or you can make excuses, but not both. Decide which side you want to be on and work at it every day.

The easiest person to lie to is yourself. So saying *"I'm not good at that"* becomes a self-fulfilling prophecy. We need to be very careful how we speak to ourselves. Start saying: "*I'm not good at that… yet.*" Let's cultivate a growth mindset and let go of any fixed-mindset beliefs.

Vision, Language & Belief

Your language creates your limits & your vision creates your direction. I recommend my mentees visualize:

- The keys in their hand
- The rent landing in their account
- The home they'll one day buy for their family

I'm not one for manifestation, but I do believe in goal-setting and having a positive mental attitude.

Write your goals down. Create short, medium, and long-term goals. Speak them aloud. Tell others, but be aware of the naysayers who will fill you with negativity. You must distance yourself from these people because they will prevent you from achieving your goals.

Declare

- "This year I'm buying a new home."

- "This year I'm buying my first/next BTL."
- "This year I'm buying a block of flats."

Remember Nelson Mandela's quote: '*Something is impossible until somebody does it*'; therefore, if one person has done it, you can too.

Start Small & Stay Consistent

You don't have to figure everything out today, just start by setting a simple goal:

- Research properties for 30 mins
- Book a viewing for this week
- Go to a networking meeting this month
- Get your first/next deal over the line
- Increase your cash flow by £1,000 per month
- Then £2,000
- Then £3,000 etc

As your property Sensei, I need to say, "*The journey of a thousand miles starts with the first step, so take one step at a time. Then keep going.*"

One of my mentees did more deals in 2022 than he had from 2013 to 2019 combined.

But it started with a single decision. Decide today to take a big step forward on your journey.

Property isn't always easy, but it's easier than spending 40 years in a job you hate and then retiring on 40% of what you used to earn. No, thank you, I'm not solely relying on the government to look after my family and me; we can do much better than that.

Rejection, Confidence & Resilience

You will get rejected and receive knockbacks. Some estate agents won't return your calls. Some people will talk down to you. Some people won't give you the time of day.

It doesn't matter. It's your job to keep getting up and keep showing up. What matters is your self-belief and determination. You only need one good agent; that one good agent can keep you busy all year. That 1 good investor can fund all your deals if you deliver on your promise.

People will try to drag you down when you start doing well. It's not personal. It's their fear speaking.

Nothing great ever came from your comfort zone. To grow into who you want to be, you must get uncomfortable. That's where the magic happens.

Your Environment Shapes You

Most people follow the blueprint they inherited from their parents, teachers, and friends. It often goes something like this: go to school, get good grades, get a good job, go on holiday for 2 weeks a year, pay off your mortgage, and retire. Sound familiar?

If you want a new outcome, then you must get into a new environment.

- Play with and against better people
- Learn from those ahead of you
- Surround yourself with investors, not spectators

You become what you're around. If you're always around comfort, you'll stay average. Enrol in a group where you will be stretched and where success is the only outcome.

Change your input, change your circle, and watch how it'll change your results.

The Wake-Up Call: Action Beats Theory

- *"I'm too busy."* → Then don't grow and stay broke
- *"I'll start next year."* → The window's closing. Every day you are missing out
- *"I can't afford mentorship."* → You can't afford not to invest in mentorship. The cost of no mentorship costs more than the mentorship

Start changing your story. If you want something different, you need to do something different. Most people sleepwalk through life, so I urge you to stop sleeping your life away. We were only here for a short time, so make it count.

Fail Fast & Fail Forward

How you do anything is how you do everything. Start small and build your daily disciplines; they will compound, and your life will head in a completely new direction.

The key isn't learning, it's implementation. I am cramming a lot of information into this book, but information isn't the key; implementation is.

Of course, you'll make mistakes at first, I still do, and every successful person does. But they fail forward, fail fast, and learn from their failures. They don't give up, they learn, adjust, and keep moving.

You're not limited by what you know. You're only limited by what you're willing to do. Develop that Unshakeable Black Belt Mindset, and you will be successful.

In Summary

Thinking like a professional investor isn't about having all the answers; it's about making the decision to start, committing fully, and building the habits and mindset that create momentum. The pros aren't always the smartest in the room, but they are the ones who act, stay resilient, and surround themselves with people who lift them higher. If you focus on consistency, growth, and implementation, success isn't a matter of *if*, it's a matter of *when*.

Chapter 10

How Inflation Makes Property Investors Wealthy?

Inflation is constant, but it's not your enemy. Smart Black Belt investors understand it and how to let it do the heavy lifting.

What Is Inflation (And Why Should You Care)?

Inflation is the gradual increase in the price of goods and services over time. Put simply, your money buys you less in the future than it does today. It's why £1'000 today will have less purchasing power 10 years from now. In under 100 years, from 1900 to 2000, £100 has lost over 99% of its buying power. That's a very scary statistic.

While inflation might seem like a problem for everyone, property investors who understand it can use it to their advantage and quietly build wealth.

Why Inflation Hurts Savers (But Helps Investors)?

When inflation is high, it's bad news for savers. Interest rates on savings accounts are often lower than the rate of inflation, which means the real value of your savings is shrinking year after year. We don't notice it, though, because the numbers on our online banking screen don't seem to change.

I'm sure if it had a 'buying power' graph next to it that clearly showed it was losing power, we would pay more attention.

But for investors with 'good debt', such as fixed-rate mortgages on income-producing properties that appreciate in value, inflation can actually be a powerful wealth-building tool.

That's because while inflation pushes prices (and rents) upward, your mortgage balance remains fixed. So over time, you're repaying the debt with money that's worth less, and your real debt load decreases.

How Inflation Quietly Builds Equity?

Here's a simple example:

Let's say you bought a house in 2008 for £100,000.

You put down a 25% deposit (£25,000) and borrowed the remaining £75,000 on a 25-year mortgage.

Fast forward 17 years to 2025. The same property is now worth £180,000, thanks to long-term market appreciation and inflation. But your mortgage is still around £75,000 (or even less, depending on your repayment schedule).

While the property value has increased, the real cost of the debt has decreased. You've gained equity from two angles:

1. Capital appreciation
2. Inflation reduces the real-world value of your debt

Meanwhile, rental income is likely to have increased over time to reflect inflation and wage growth, helping you maintain or even grow your cash flow.

The figures above are for 1 of our properties, and this is the silent power of inflation. It chips away at the value of your debt while boosting the value of your assets. If you are a parent and want your children to be financially savvy, teach them so they have a helping hand in understanding how the real world works.

The Risk: When Inflation Isn't Your Friend?

Of course, inflation isn't all upside. Higher inflation often leads to higher interest rates, which can:

- Eat into your monthly cash flow
- Increase the cost of borrowing
- Reduce the affordability of further investments

Over-leveraged investors, sometimes referred to as over-geared (i.e., with high loan-to-value ratios), and have low cash flow are especially vulnerable.

How To Protect Yourself And Still Win?

To ensure you benefit from inflation; rather than get burned by it, follow these best practices:

- Lock in fixed interest rates where possible (especially during low-rate periods)

- Buy properties with strong cash flow, don't rely on capital growth alone
- Keep cash reserves to cover rising costs or void periods
- Stress-test your deals at higher interest rates before committing
- Think long-term; inflation rewards patience, not panic

In Summary

Inflation is one of the most powerful forces in the economy, and it's inevitable; however, if you understand how to use it, it can quietly make you rich over time. By securing good debt, buying cash-flowing properties, and holding for the long term, inflation works in your favour. Your debt erodes, your rents rise, and your assets appreciate. But if you overstretch yourself or ignore rising interest rates, inflation can quickly turn from friend to foe. Are you going to be one of the investors who benefit from it?

Chapter 11

Mentorship Matters...Kaizen

You can try to figure it all out alone, or you can accelerate your success with the right mentorship. The choice is yours.

Let me keep this short and honest, I wouldn't be where I am today without mentors.

One of the greatest accelerators in my journey, whether in Karate, Martial Arts Business, or Property Investing, has been mentorship.

Even as a 'reasonable' 6th Degree Black Belt and 'fairly' successful property investor, I still have a Sensei who is a higher grade than me and still invest in mentorship because you *'don't know what you don't know'*. Olympic athletes have coaches, so why shouldn't we?

Yes, you can learn through trial and error. I did for years, but looking back, I could've shortcut a lot of pain, time, and money if I had learned from people who were already where I wanted to go. I had a true *"I'm not paying for mentorship"* mindset, and it cost me at least £250,000 in lost profit and probably £500,000 in lost wealth (maybe even more). Don't make my mistake.

Real growth came when I humbled myself, sought expert guidance, and invested in mentorship. I'd be much further ahead if I'd acted sooner instead of sitting on the fence.

Why I Believe So Strongly In Mentorship?

In both martial arts and business, I've always followed the principle of Kaizen, *the way of continual improvement.*

Kaizen is about making consistent, small steps forward; day after day, year after year. It's not about perfection; it's about progress. That mindset is the backbone of everything we teach in the **Black Belt Property Academy**.

Over the years, I've taught over 10,000 martial arts students and personally guided more than 500 to Black Belt. That's not just about kicks and punches, it's about mindset, discipline, and long-term growth. In the **Black Belt Property Academy**, I bring that same teaching philosophy to property investing.

At the **Black Belt Property Academy**, we take complete beginners and *White Belt investors*, and give them the structure, support, and systems to grow to Black Belt and beyond. Just like in martial arts, success in property is about setting goals and consistent progress, not overnight results.

If you've been trying to figure it all out alone, stop. You don't need to. Learn from someone who's taken hundreds from *"zero" to "master"*, and is ready to help you do the same.

If you want to accelerate your growth, find someone who's walked the path before you. Learn from their mistakes, borrow their mindset, and copy what works.

"Success leaves clues. Follow them."

If you're serious about taking your life or business to the next level, ask yourself the following: Am I investing in myself as much as I could be?

If you're wondering where to start, I've included a detailed section at the back of this book on how to get involved in mentorship, if you're ready to take action. You'll find details on the **Black Belt Property Academy**, how it works, and whether we're the right fit.

You don't have to go it alone.

In Summary

Mentorship is not a luxury. It's a shortcut, a multiplier, a decision that separates the dabblers from the doers. You are leveraging somebody else's experience to help you grow. Yes, you can go far alone, but you'll go further and much faster with the right guidance.

More on the **Black Belt Property Academy** at the end of the book.

Chapter 12

The Amateur Vs The Professional: Which One Are You?

Amateurs play safe, buy 1-3 properties, and manage every detail themselves. Professionals think big, add value, leverage strategies, and build scalable cash-flowing portfolios. Which one are you ready to be?

I think we need to establish here that you can be in whichever camp you choose. As I did, you might start as an amateur but then become a professional investor over time. I'm not talking about experience when I say '*amateur or professional*', I'm talking about how you approach your investment journey. The fact that you have invested in this book and have read it so far means you already have the characteristics of a professional investor.

Below are some characteristics of amateur and professional investors.

The Amateur Investor

- Will buy a house and then save up for their next deposit
- Look at capital growth as the only metric

- Buys perfect house on perfect street in perfect area in perfect condition
- Looks at timing the market (it's about time 'in' the market, not 'timing' the market)
- Try to do it all themselves, i.e., manage the property and maintenance
- Don't utilize leverage as well as they could
- Thinks small

The average investor buys 1-3 properties in their lifetime. They often use only 1 strategy and are typical landlords.

The Professional Investor

- Locks in profit from day 1
- Buys the worst house on an average street
- Buys a house and does a £10-15k refurb but have increased value by +£30k or more
- Don't buy cheap houses; they buy houses where they can add value
- Think what it's going to be worth when they are finished with the refurb
- Don't look at the cost of the shovel when digging for gold
- Leaves as little money in the property as possible and moves on to the next quickly
- May have a main strategy but also implement 1-2 other strategies such as Flips or SA
- Understand compounding and inflation

- Thinks big
- They have a strong mindset
- They continually learn (often through a mentor who is further on in the journey than they are)

There is a massive difference between an old-school landlord and a professional property investor. The main difference will be that the professional investor will have greater wealth and higher levels of monthly cash flow. Back in 2007, I was well and truly the amateur investor (although I didn't know it). I did everything I could to save money, but it's a false economy. I had a full-time job as a lecturer at the time and was building my Karate School up 6 days a week (evenings and Saturdays). I was the old-school landlord; I handled tenancy set-ups, collected rent, cleaned out the properties, organised maintenance, etc. This was before I knew anything about high-value and low-value tasks, and how to build and systemise a business. Not surprisingly, this was before any form of mentoring.

In the **Black Belt Property Academy**, we help mentees evolve into becoming professional investors. If you are getting into property just to have 2-3 BTLs. Then, of course, it's better than nothing, but with a professional mindset and solid knowledge, it could easily be 10 properties, a combination of HMOs and BTLs. You just need to learn to execute your main strategy and then refine it each time. You could have a great cash-flowing portfolio with 99% passive income, and the rent just lands in your account every month. Don't be fooled into thinking you will be financially free with 5 BTLs; they are great, but BTLs are slow wealth builders; they are not the high cash-flowing asset. Having 5-10 BTLs is a great position to be in, but you aren't going to retire on the cash flow they provide.

Associate With Positive People

You become the sum of the people you surround yourself with. Likewise, if you hang around with clowns, expect a circus, so surround yourself with like-minded people, i.e., people who want to go places and who want to achieve great things. Don't get your property advice from your family, who are non-investors; get it from your property family.

In Summary

Thinking like a professional investor isn't about having all the answers; it's about deciding to start, committing fully, and building the habits and mindset that create momentum. Professionals don't need to be the smartest in the room; they're the ones who take action, stay resilient, and surround themselves with people who lift them higher. Amateurs wait and play it safe; professionals add value, build systems, and think bigger. Nobody is born a pro; you grow into one by learning, adapting, and implementing consistently. With the right mindset, support, and focus, success isn't if, it's when. The choice is yours: stay average, or become exceptional.

Chapter 13

Commitment: The First Deal Is With Yourself

Commit to yourself fully before making your first property deal, real success comes from unwavering dedication and persistent action, not just interest. When you're truly committed, opportunities and support naturally follow.

Before you make your first offer, view your first property, or calculate a single metric, there's one deal you must make, and it's not with a seller, a broker, or a bank. It's with yourself.

Property investing isn't just about numbers or knowing the right strategies. It's about showing up when you don't feel like it, pushing forward when things get tough, and following through when distractions and doubts creep in. That takes commitment, not half-hearted interest but real, full-blooded commitment.

One of my favourite quotes, from Scottish mountaineer W.H. Murray, captures this perfectly:

> **"Until one is committed, there is hesitancy, the chance to draw back, always ineffectiveness.**

Concerning all acts of initiative (and creation), there is one elementary truth the ignorance of which kills countless ideas and splendid plans:

That is the moment one definitely commits oneself, then Providence moves too.

All sorts of things occur to help one that would never otherwise have occurred..."

When you're truly committed, the right knowledge, people, and opportunities start showing up. Not because they magically appear, but because you've tuned your mind and actions to spot them, pursue them, and be ready for them.

Don't play the 'interested' game; make sure you are all in.

The most successful investors I've mentored aren't always the most talented or well-connected, but they are fully committed, and that's a huge plus for their success journey. They learn relentlessly, implement quickly, build strong networks, raise finance, and move forward despite challenges. They play to win, and in doing so, they build portfolios that give their families long-term security and freedom. That's what we want for all the mentees on our **Black Belt Property Academy.**

Back in 2015, I had a modest property portfolio. Since I had a successful karate school, I was doing okay, but I wasn't really committed to the property side of our business. I had knowledge I hadn't used. I had strategies I hadn't executed. My success was stalling, not because I lacked opportunity, but because I hadn't truly decided to go all in. Don't make my mistake.

If you're serious about building wealth through property, you need more than goals; you need a plan, a vision, and the commitment to stay in the game when things don't go your way.

Because at some point, you'll run out of money, hit a wall, or face doubt. And its commitment that will carry you through to the next level.

JOB = Just Over Broke; Robert Kiyosaki

Don't settle for 'just over broke' in a job you hate. Commit to building your financial future now and watch how everything begins to shift in your favour.

In Summary

Every property journey starts with a decision, and the most important deal you'll ever make is the one you make with yourself. When you stop dabbling and commit fully, you move from interested to invested, and that shift is what separates those who succeed from those who stay stuck. With real commitment, progress becomes inevitable, not optional.

Chapter 14

How To Profit From The Property Cycle? (Not Be Crushed By It)

The property market moves in cycles; understanding these phases helps you buy low, sell high, and avoid costly mistakes. By recognizing where we are in the cycle, you can make smarter investment decisions, build cash flow, and protect your portfolio through ups and downs.

Like most things in life, there is a pattern. The property cycle is a pattern. When my mentees understand the property cycle, it undoubtedly helps them make better investment decisions. Understanding the property cycle will give you an investor's edge.

The property cycle is the pattern that property values take over a set period of time. In its simplest terms, if property prices increase, there is then a correction where prices dip (the mid-cycle dip), the property increases again at a quicker rate than before, and then a bigger dip occurs (the recession phase). The lowest point of the 2nd dip has always been higher than the lowest point in the previous dip.

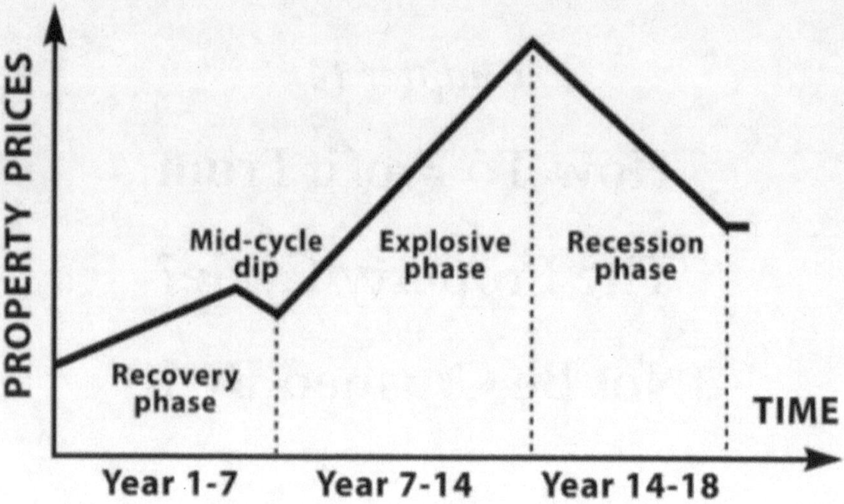

The property cycle tends to last approximately. 18 years (18.2 to be precise), and there are 4 main parts of the cycle: recovery phase, mid-cycle dip, explosive phase, and recession phase.

Investors who understand the cycle know that in the long run, property values always increase. If you are a *'buy and hold forever'* investor, you could argue that the purchase price is somewhat irrelevant because in 20, 30, or 50 years, the price will be much higher than what you paid.

Prices do not increase linearly. Some years' growth might be quite stagnant, others may be in double digits, and in others, the price may dip. Don't listen to the doom and gloom in the media. Their job is to catch eyeballs, and negative stories sell far more than positive ones do.

If your portfolio is cash-flowing positively, the property's value does not necessarily matter. Warren Buffett says that if he buys a stock and it immediately goes down, he then buys even more because he knows he has invested in a strong business and in the long run it will recover. The most professional investors buy as much property as they can at the bottom of the market.

Why do prices go up? It's often because there are not that many houses available, i.e., supply and demand. However, as more houses become available on the market, you will see prices dip because now buyers have much more choice. Prices will not always go up; they will inevitably come down at some point.

Be Fearful When Others Are Greedy And Greedy When Others Are Fearful

As investors, we should heed Mr. Buffett's advice. Many seasoned professional investors start to calm down their buying activity when in the final stages of the boom phase, only to resume when property prices have crashed. Buying at the lowest phase means yields are great, and you are picking up prime assets at a 'special offer' discount. I tell my children that it's like houses are on special offer. I need them to understand the Property Cycle.

Recovery Phase

Prices have now dropped to their lowest and are now slowly but surely on their way back up. Nobody actually knows where the bottom is, so you need to study prices and keep an eye on them weekly to see which way the trend is leaning. Selling at the bottom is the worst thing to do; I nearly did it with my little portfolio of 3 houses back in 2009. I am so glad I didn't because I would have crystallised my losses and regretted it for many years.

The recovery phase is the best time to buy because properties are undervalued, and competition is low. However, this is also when lenders tighten up their criteria, so it becomes harder, not impossible, to lend.

Prices start to increase as more people buy. When banks make it easier to lend money, property prices start to increase. One of my early mentors used to say that as soon as you see big, crazy building projects underway, you know you are in the explosive phase. When there are more houses for sale than buyers, then you know it's a dip.

Let's remember, though, that the prices will not always continue to rise, it's a cycle.

A buyer's market is when there are more properties than buyers (low prices)

A seller's market is when there are more buyers than properties (high prices)

The Expansion Phase

Confidence has returned to the market, and there has been rapid price growth. You will notice that properties don't stay on the market for too long before a sale price has been agreed. Investors at all stages need to be aware of overpaying, but especially during this phase of the cycle.

The Hyper Supply Phase

The price of property is still on the rise, but when tracked more diligently, the rate of growth has slowed. Investors do not want to purchase at this stage because this is the highest price the property will be for many years. This is a great time to sell underperforming assets; you can bank the money and then re-invest during the recession phase.

The Winner's Curse

A term coined by Fred Harrison is when you overpay for a property just before the recession, and it's not long before it's worth far less than what you have paid. Don't get sucked into the winner's phase.

Recession

This is where every media source reports that property is crashing and scaring people with questions like '*will the housing market ever recover?*' Lending obviously becomes a lot tighter during this phase. This phase is excellent for investors with access to capital; they can buy great assets at a bargain price. Investing, though, should be based on rational, not emotional, considerations. During this phase, you need to understand the numbers and the cycle's stages fully.

I urge you to learn more about the property cycle so that you can read the signs of when things are good and bad. Things are never as good as you think they are, and things are never as bad as you think they are.

The cycle might not be 18 years; it might be shorter or longer, but as a professional investor, you need to know that it will happen. If the last one was 2009, then the next one should be approximately. 2025, but we had a global pandemic in 2020, which has thrown a spanner in the works. The main thing is that you are now aware of the property cycle and can make a more informed decision on your investments.

During the explosive phase, some investors analyse their portfolio and decide to sell some properties that no longer meet their needs. They then reinvest the money in better properties purchased during the recession phase.

Should I Wait For The Next Crash?

No, because there is an opportunity cost to doing that. You may be able to secure a great BMV deal and benefit from the cash flow for 1-2-3 years before the crash. If you are a '*buy and hold forever*' investor, you know that, in the long run, it will all work out. Again, that is why it's crucial to lock in profit from day 1.

Unlike stocks, to my knowledge, the price of property has never gone to zero.

If you have a good relationship with local agents, you would still be touching base with them and making offers on properties you know have been on the market for a long time.

In Summary

Knowing that prices will not always go up or down is a step in the right direction. The more you understand about the property cycle and can recognise the signs, the better an investor you will be. Your cash flow will be more secure, and your portfolio will not be over geared.

Chapter 15

Speak The Language: Property Acronyms You Need To Know

Property investing comes with many acronyms, such as BMV, ROI, ROCE, HMO, and more. They may seem confusing at first, but understanding them is key to making smart investment decisions.

In the property investing world, there are many acronyms thrown around all the time. Most investors use them when needed, but a few like to use them as if it's a special secret language and to gauge your knowledge. Don't be fooled. Knowing what these acronyms mean will help you along your journey.

If you have read books, magazines, watched YouTube videos, and I hope, subscribed to my channel, or listened to podcasts, you are likely to have come across many of these already. BMV, PP, ROI, ROCE, to name just a few. To a beginner just starting their journey, it can seem quite overwhelming. Don't worry, we were all beginners once; we are all just on different stages of the journey. I always tell my students, *'Somebody had to teach Bruce Lee how to kick, and somebody had to teach Muhammad Ali how to box.'*

This section explains some of the main acronyms you will come across when you start your property investing journey; it's not intended to be a full A-Z of property language.

BMV = Below Market Value

Meaning that you have purchased it below the 'perceived' market value. For example, the property is up for sale for £150k, and you purchased it for £135k; that would be a 'BMV' deal, as investors, you always want to get BMV deals. Black Belt investors lock in profit from day 1.

PP = Purchase Price

This is not the agreed sale price. When I calculate PP, I like to include all the legal fees and Stamp Duty. Whatever it has cost me to get the keys, I consider it as PP. Some investors actually just classify the PP as the sale price, which, in my opinion, is wrong.

SSTC = Sold Subject To Contract

This is a term estate agents use when a property has been sold, and it's in the conveyancing stage. The property, though, is not sold until contracts have been exchanged.

LTV = Loan To Value

When purchasing property with a mortgage as an investor, you will need to put down a 25% deposit, with the remaining 75% as your LTV. If you purchase a £100k property and put in a 25k deposit, your loan-to-value is 75%, i.e., 75% of the purchase price.

GDV – Gross Development Value

This is the estimated total value of the property once all works are done. The term GDV is often used when extensive refurbishment is being carried out, i.e., flips, conversions, and commercial property. Knowing your end value or GDV is essential for your BRRR planning.

ILA = Independent Legal Advice

If you are buying through a LTD company, you often need to seek independent legal advice. The solicitor you use for the ILA will explain to you that if you fail to pay the mortgage, you will personally be held responsible (see PG below)

PG = Personal Guarantee

When taking part in your ILA, the solicitor will ask you to complete a PG at the request of the lender. This is so you are under no illusion that if you close down your company or it fails to pay, you will be personally held responsible.

ROI = Return On Investment

This is a common business metric indicating how much return you anticipate relative to the amount of money you invest. If you put in £25k and are going to NET £2.5k each year, that's a 10% ROI (£2.5k / £25k = 10%). Personally, I prefer to look at ROCE, which I will cover later. ROI is a very relevant metric because something could cost £100k and return £15k per year, which is 15% ROI, or it could cost the same £100k and return £2k per year, which is a terrible 2% ROI (still better than most savings accounts though).

AST = Assured Shorthold Tenancy

This is a tenancy agreement that residential tenants sign when they move into a house (or bedroom if you are investing in HMOs) in England. NEVER let your property/rooms out without a correct agreement. We made this silly mistake between 2007 and 2010, and it cost us ££££. An AST is the standard tenancy used in England. You do not need an AST if you are choosing to run SA units, since you don't have tenants; you have guests.

BRR = Buy, Refurbish, Rent

This is a common property-investing strategy, mainly for long-term gains. You purchase the property, aim to add value, and then rent it out.

BRRR = Buy, Refurbish, Refinance, Rent

A common strategy for investors wanting to recycle their funds, allowing them to scale their portfolio quickly. It's the same as BRR, but often with more refurbishment, creating more value, allowing you to pull more money from the property to invest in another. This is a main pillar of our property investing strategy.

BTL = Buy To Let

You are buying the property with the intention of letting it out (rather than 'flipping' or refinancing).

SA = Serviced Accommodation

Property available for short and medium-term lets. The property is fully furnished and will include cleaning services. It would be like a 'home from home.'

HMO = House Of Multiple Occupation

This is where tenants rent a room and share certain communal areas. Most HMOs offer an all-inclusive rent that includes bills, internet, etc, often referred to as a multi-let property. These are a great strategy to have a higher level of cash flow each month.

JV = Joint Venture

This is when you work with someone to share the benefits that property investment can bring.1 person may provide the funds, while the other provides contacts, experience, etc. A JV can have more than 2 people. A JV is a partnership.

ERC = Early Repayment Charge

Your mortgage lender will impose an ERC to ensure they are paid during your tied-in period. If you have a 5-year fixed mortgage, you are likely to pay a fee or penalty equal to % of the loan amount if you leave the mortgage early. It may be 5% in year 1, 4% in year 2, 3% in year 3, and so on.

R2R = Rent-To-Rent

When you take control of a property (legally) without owning it, but then rent the property out. You keep the difference between what you pay the owner and what the tenants pay you. This is not adverse possession, and R2R is legal when done properly.

SDLT = Stamp Duty Land Tax

One of my personal favourite taxes to pay, I love it! This is the money you pay to HMRC based on the value of the property you are purchasing and the condition of the property. You must always consider SDLT when stacking a deal. If the numbers don't work, then move on. Never force the numbers to work.

OPM = Other People's Money

A term used when you are using other people's money (OPM) to invest in property. You can arrange to borrow money from them and pay a higher interest rate than what they are currently getting. A mortgage is OPM; you just need to put down a 25% deposit first, which could come from OPM (however most lenders want to see bank statements to check where the money has come from).

CGT = Capital Gains Tax

This is the tax you will pay when you sell the property on any uplift from what you paid for the property to what you sold it for. If you are educated, there are many expenses you can offset to reduce CGT, so it's not all bad news.

DPC = Damp Proof Course

Work carried out to prevent rising damp. You can have a DPC in 1 area, e.g, your kitchen, or you can have a DPC across all your ground floor.

EPC = Energy Performance Certificate

This is another brilliant piece of legislation that the government brought in. It is a measure of how energy-efficient your property is. For instance, a house with single-glazed windows, no loft insulation, and no central heating system would rate much lower than a property with triple glazing, 50mm of loft insulation, and a triple A-grade central heating system. When purchasing through a mortgage, the property will need an EPC certificate.

SARB = Sale And Rent Back

This is where a vendor sells their property to a company and then rents it back from them. There were some very scrupulous companies that, upon buying the properties, wouldn't let the vendors rent it back, charged very high, or let them rent for 12 months at a competitive rate and then spiked it up, forcing them to move out.

PD = Permitted Development

Your local government sets guidelines on how far you can extend your house before having to get planning permission. You are allowed to do certain work without needing planning permission. PD is a step before planning permission and is a much quicker process than applying for full PP.

D2V = Direct To Vendor

When you are dealing with the vendor for the sale, rather than through an estate agent, D2V is where the best deals are found because they don't need to pay estate agent fees and are often more open to conditions.

Leasehold

This is when you lease the land the property is on. You will often find that leases are for 999 years or less. Properties with short leases, for instance, 75 years remaining, are often hard to get a mortgage on. You often find that in the conveyancing stage, they take longer to get over the line than freehold.

Freehold

This is when the property you have purchased owns the land in which it sits. We like freehold properties.

Section 21

This is a notice you give to tenants explaining that you would like them to move out. There does not need to be a reason, but if you wanted to sell your property, you would need to serve a section 21 notice.

Section 24

Ok, so not really an acronym, but when you own property in your personal name (as opposed to a company structure), you cannot offset the interest of the loan/mortgage as an expense against your profit, which makes it look like you are earning more money than you actually are, crazy. All the properties I purchased back in 2007-2010 were in my personal name, so it appears I earn a lot from them when really, I don't. Yet again, another way the government can take money from you.

Section 42

If you own or want to purchase a leasehold property, you may hear the phrase 'Section 42', (often served when there is not much time left on the lease). A section 42 is sent to the freeholder requesting an extension of the lease. The lease can then be extended by 90 years.

Article 4

Again, not an acronym, but it does get mentioned a lot in property; this is where your local council has restricted any Permitted Development (PD) rights. Always research your area to check for any Article 4 restrictions, especially if you are looking at doing HMOs.

HVT's

You won't hear this in property circles, but you will hear it in entrepreneurial circles: HVTs are High Value Tasks. As a property investor, 20% of where you spend your time will bring in 80% of your profits. It's your job to drill deep into that 20% and expand the amount of time you spend there.

In Summary

Property acronyms might seem overwhelming at first, but understanding them is crucial to speaking the language of professional investors. The more fluent you become, the more confident and credible you'll feel, whether you're talking to brokers, agents, investors, or solicitors. Don't get intimidated by jargon; learn it, use it, and let it empower your journey.

Chapter 16

Personal Vs LTD Company: Which Structure Is Right For You?

Should you buy property in your personal name or an LTD company? LTD companies often offer lower tax rates and better growth potential. Always consult a property-savvy accountant, but in my experience, starting with an LTD company is the smarter choice.

People ask me this question a lot. It goes something like this: "*I'm thinking of getting into property, but should I buy in my personal name or an LTD company?*" It is then followed by something like "*a LTD company seems like a lot of hassle, but I don't know what to do…I don't want to pay even more tax.*"

Let me repeat it: I am not a financial advisor, accountant, or tax advisor. What I say is based solely on my own experience, and I will always advise you to seek professional advice.

I would always recommend people start a LTD company rather than invest in their own name, but like always, speak to a good property accountant and tell them your situation and desired goals. I would not speak to somebody with no property investing experience; try to speak to somebody who is further along in their journey than you are, i.e., they have 10-20-50 properties.

Many people start with a personal name and then go to a LTD company. That's what I did back in 2007. I'm not saying that's the best way to do it, but the tax goal posts were different back then. There was no 'section 24' (remember this from the acronym section), which meant my mortgage payments could be offset as an expense (and rightly so). Many of the old school 'landlords' bought in their name and as the rules evolve and their margins shrink, they often leave the game. This is an opportunity for you.

I have 4 properties in my personal name, and if I could turn back time, I would indeed have purchased right away in a LTD company. You don't know what you don't know, which is why we always need to keep learning. At some point, I will try to shift them into a LTD company, but I need to do it in the most tax-efficient way possible. Of course, I understand that I need to pay tax, but I don't want to pay any more than I need to. At the time of writing here in the UK, the Chancellor of the Exchequer has just avoided a £40k SDLT bill. I very much doubt she will be going to prison or have to pay for it. Imagine if that were anybody else. Ensure you run your property business as ethically and above board as you can.

Lower Tax Bill

The main reason people purchase through a LTD company is that they will pay a lower tax rate. Currently, at the time of writing, the corporation tax in the UK is 19-25% depending on the level of your turnover. I expect that if you have a handful of properties, you will be making less than £50k pa in profit, so that you will pay 19% tax.

Personal income tax is 20-40% so if all your properties are in your name, you will pay more in tax since the rent collected is treated as income. Some investors purchase properties in their spouse's name who earns less than they do, so there is less tax to pay, but rather than go through all that, seek professional advice to see if a LTD company is the best for you.

Is Setting Up A LTD Company Hard?

No, it isn't. You can make property investing as easy or as hard as you like. One of the concepts we teach to mentees is '*who, not how*'. If you want to sell a house, you don't carry out the legal work; you employ a solicitor. If you are having open heart surgery, you have a trained person. Always think '*who*' do I get to do this, not '*how*' do I do this.

I have set up companies before; I just ask my accountant to do it, I get a confirmation email, and that's it. Of course, there is a cost, and you can do it yourself for a fraction of what a professional would charge, but I value my time and want to make sure it's all set up properly. Personally, I would also make sure that your registered office is the accountant's office. Back in 2007-2012, I had everything sent to my home address, and trust me, this is not the best practice. I started to develop a fear of opening letters, especially the brown HMRC ones (a 6th Degree Karate Black Belt scared of opening letters!).

Trading History

When I first started out, I was obsessed with not having any trading history. As a result, I wrongly delayed setting up a proper business account and a LTD company. This was backward thinking. There are companies out there that earn money by lending you money. You can set up a LTD company and apply for a mortgage the day after. Don't say that you can't get a mortgage because you haven't got 12 months' worth of accounts. If you speak to a broker who says you need 2 years' accounts, speak to another broker; there is always a way.

The Best Accountants

I would always advise going to an accountant who invests in property themselves. I'm not talking about 1 * BTL property because they are often 'accidental landlords'; I'm talking about somebody who has a growing portfolio and can guide you through the sometimes-murky waters. When I first set up my LTD company, I wrongly just went to an accountant who did my friend's accounts because he said he was good. Please don't do that. Work with an accountant who has many property investor clients and ideally invests in property themselves. They should save you far more in tax than the amount you pay them; don't step over pounds to pick up pennies.

In Summary

In my experience, setting up an LTD company has been the best route. A personal name can be easier and often offers cheaper interest rates, but there may be higher tax implications further down the line. Just to clarify again, please seek professional advice from your accountant or tax advisor.

Chapter 17

Tax, Accounting & Structures, Get This Right Early

Getting your tax, accounting, and business structure right from day one is the difference between building real wealth and handing your profits straight to the taxman. Plan smart, track everything, and surround yourself with the right experts to keep more of what you earn.

I'll start with this: I'm not a qualified accountant or tax advisor. What I'll share here is from my own journey and what I've learned working with great professionals. Please speak to an accountant or similar professional before making any tax decisions. That said, I wish I had known half of this when I started…

Why Tax Knowledge Is A Superpower In Property?

You might be able to pick up bargain properties and buy extremely well throughout your journey, but if you're handing your profits straight to the taxman, what's the point?

Your property investing journey should be about legally keeping more of what you earn.

For Example:

I have four properties in my personal name, and I pay significantly more tax on them compared to the rest of my portfolio. According to HMRC, all the rent from those properties is 100% profit. Back in 2007, when I started, most people didn't buy in a company; they bought in their personal name.

But now, with Section 24 in place, you can no longer offset mortgage interest against your profits (which is absolutely ridiculous, by the way). Section 24 is the UK tax rule that gradually removed the ability for landlords who owned properties in their own name, to deduct mortgage interest from their rental income. So while the actual income from those properties is maybe half of what it looks like, the taxman sees something very different:

£1,125 + £600 + £750 + £850 = £3,325 per month = £39,900 per year.

Even if your actual profit is half of that due to mortgage payments, HMRC will want tax on the full amount. This is why your structure matters, especially early on. You need to build the right foundations.

It's not all bad news, though. In the UK, you can claim *mortgage interest relief* on properties that you own in your personal name. Don't get too excited just yet, however. Unlike properties owned through a LTD company, where all mortgage interest can be deducted as an expense, properties held in your personal name only qualify for a 20% tax credit on the mortgage interest. This doesn't reduce your rental income or your profit; instead, the tax credit is applied directly to your tax bill, reducing the amount of income tax you pay. So, although you can't deduct the full mortgage interest, you do still receive a 20% tax credit against your overall tax bill. That's a little silver lining at least.

Let's be clear: I'm not telling you to do anything illegal. What I'm saying is plan properly so all your hard-earned income and wealth don't disappear to taxes. Wealth isn't just what you earn, it's what you keep and how you structure it.

Personal Name Vs Limited Company

I won't go over this in detail again (we've covered it earlier in the book), but it's worth repeating:

Your decision on whether to buy in your personal name or through a limited company should be based on your long-term goals.

In many cases, buying in a Ltd company is more tax efficient, but this is not a one-size-fits-all decision. Speak to a trusted accountant and explain what you want to achieve.

Basic Accounting & Bookkeeping Habits

Property investing or not, you should track your income and expenses monthly.

People who don't understand cash flow rarely build successful, profitable businesses (unless they employ someone who does).

You should create a simple spreadsheet that records all your property-related expenses:

- Mortgage payments
- Bridging finance fees
- Broker fees
- Educational costs
- Networking events

- Trade magazine subscriptions
- Fuel
- Ground rent…and so on.

The last thing you want is to show the taxman that you're collecting rent but have no expenses to report. Doing so will result in a higher tax bill than needed. We advise all mentees to track all rental income, including arrears or partial payments. This helps identify problems early and keeps you HMRC-compliant.

Again, I'm not suggesting anything illegal, but offset any legitimate, legal expense you incur while running your property business.

There are apps and cloud systems you can use, like QuickBooks or Xero, which let you snap receipts and track expenses automatically. But I always recommend our mentees start with a basic spreadsheet and get into the habit of updating it weekly. As your portfolio grows, this becomes less of a high-value task and should be delegated, allowing you to focus on the tasks that move the needle most in your business.

Once you do, you'll know your numbers inside-out, and that makes you dangerous (in a good way). Property is a business, and you must treat it like one from day one.

What You Can & Can't Claim?

As of January 2026, here are some allowable expenses; always check current guidelines and speak to a professional.

Common Allowable Expenses

- Letting agent fees

- Mortgage interest (if using a Ltd Company)
- Repairs and maintenance
- Service charges
- Insurance
- Council tax (if you're covering it between tenants)
- Mileage for property viewings or inspections
- Accountancy fees

Capital Expenses (Not Immediately Claimable, But Can Add To Property Value):

- Renovations that improve the property
- Extensions
- Brand-new kitchens/bathrooms (if upgrades)

A good way to remember whether it's a repair or a capital improvement; fixing a broken tap, that's classed as a repair. Installing a new kitchen, that's a capital improvement.

Depreciation & Capital Allowances

You may not need to worry about this right now, but it's good to be familiar with the terms.

In the UK, unlike in the US, residential property investors can't claim depreciation like in other countries (be careful what YouTubers are telling you; they're not always UK-based). You cannot claim depreciation on the building itself for tax purposes.

If you're investing in commercial property, you may be able to claim Capital Allowances, but this is a more advanced topic.

We go deeper into this inside the **Black Belt Property Academy**, but if you're early in your journey, don't lose sleep over it.

Work With Your Accountant

This could be one of the most important points in this chapter:

Find an accountant who understands property, or better yet, one who actually invests themselves. Most accountants can handle property tax in theory, but those who are actively investing will understand the nuances and save you money. Do not just employ a 'bean counter' style accountant (apologies to any accountants reading this), employing an accountant who is an active property investor will pay for itself over and over again.

If your accountant doesn't invest, it's okay to keep looking. Ask them directly:

"Do you invest in property yourself?" If they say no, then politely move on. You're not being rude, you're building your Power Team, and you need the right people in your corner if you are serious about growth.

Book a free consultation with a few property-savvy accountants. Ask them what kind of clients they serve. Get a feel for whether they understand your goals.

Your accountant should:

- Understand your goals
- Help you structure your business
- Help you legally reduce tax liabilities
- Meet with you at least annually (ideally every 6 months)

Accountants can save or cost you thousands, so make sure you choose wisely.

Wealth Structuring: Think Long-Term

This might not apply to you right now, but again, let's think like professionals.

You may hear these terms at networking events or from more advanced investors:

- Holding companies
- Family Investment Companies (FICs)
- Trusts
- Inheritance tax planning
- Life insurance strategies
- Building generational wealth

Most of this is for later down the line, but awareness now gives you options later. If you are at the start of your journey now, then plan to look at this in year 2 or year 3. We must structure our property business today so that our future self can say thank you.

In Summary

Plan for tax from day one, don't wait until year-end. Set up a simple, accurate bookkeeping system and keep it up to date. Learn the difference between revenue and capital expenses. Your accountant can be a huge asset if they know what they're doing. The goal isn't just to make money, it's to keep more of it, legally. Think beyond today, structure your wealth for the long game.

PART 3

Proven Strategies For Property Success

There are many ways to make money in property, but not every strategy suits every investor, and not all of them stand the test of time. In this section, we break down the most reliable, proven strategies, from Buy to Let and HMOs to Flips, Serviced Accommodation, and more. You'll learn what each strategy involves, its pros and cons, and how to choose the right approach based on your goals, resources, and risk profile. This isn't just about learning tactics; it's about thinking strategically, building a model that works for you, and becoming a Black Belt investor.

Chapter 18

The Core Property Strategies (And When To Use Them)

Mastering the right property strategy is your fastest route to consistent wealth; choose wisely, execute flawlessly, and watch your portfolio soar. Jumping between shiny new tactics without focus will cost you time, money, and confidence.

There are many ways to make money in property. You have the classic 'buy and rent' model or the 'buy and sell' model, and then many others in between. Below are just some ways you can make money in property. You must remember, though, that to be successful in any strategy, you need to learn about it in depth, so many people fall for '*shinny penny syndrome*', they do a little BTL, then try SA, then move to HMO, etc. The strategy you go for should always link back to your '*why*' – why are you investing in property? If you answer that, then you are ½ way there.

Buy To Let

What Is BTL?

This is the most traditional way of investing in property. It's simply where you buy a property and then rent it out. If you think of an old school landlord, this is traditionally what strategy they use.

How It Works?

You save up or borrow from an investor 25% deposit for the property. You then purchase and rent it out ASAP. The tenants pay you each month, and that money should comfortably cover your interest-only mortgage payment. You can do the BRRR strategy for BTL, but you often purchase it through bridging finance first.

Why BTL?

In the long run, the money you invested is growing at a better rate than in the bank, plus if done properly, you are receiving positive cash flow every month, and it's tenanted. The best reason for us is that we have a fixed debt against an appreciating asset that pays us every month its tenanted.

Ideal BTL

You pick it up at BMW, it needs a minor refurb, you can pull almost all/most of your money back out, and you have a cash-producing asset with a fixed debt.

Advantages

- ✓ Simple to understand
- ✓ Cash flow each month
- ✓ Capital Growth
- ✓ Lower management requirements compared to HMO and SA
- ✓ A large number of lenders to choose from

Disadvantages & Risks

Lower cash flow compared to HMO or SA

It's either 100% empty or 100% full; there is no buffer when it's empty (unlike HMOs or MUFBs)

- × Void periods cost you money
- × Having a tenant who does not pay
- × Having a tenant who neglects the house
- × Section 24 increases tax if held in a personal name

As a property investor, I believe having a firm foundation of simple, 'boring', vanilla BTLs is a must. It's the generational wealth piece of your investing puzzle. We occasionally deal in flips and might look at the SA route moving forward, but I don't think anybody should underestimate the long-term benefits BTLs have.

Flipping

What Is Flipping?

You buy a property and then sell it, aiming to make a profit.

How It Works?

Most of the time, you carry out a level of refurbishment to add value; the uplift in value minus the associated buying, selling, conveyancing, holding, and refurbishment costs is your profit. Your profit will be subject to income tax or corporation tax, depending on how you purchased the property. The property you purchase might not need any work, or it does need work, but you choose to flip it without doing anything because you purchased it at a great price.

Why Flip?

Lots of investors who want to build a portfolio flip property, and then the profit gained gets invested in a property they want to keep in their portfolio.

Ideal Flip

Purchased at a great price (30-40% BMV), you can add value 100% in line with your end user, the market increases during your refurb, you sell at a great profit margin, i.e., £25k upwards.

Advantages

- ✓ Nice lumps of cash when done properly
- ✓ No long-term tenant management
- ✓ Clear exit strategy

Disadvantages & Risks

- × Needs significant upfront capital
- × Refurb costs might go over budget and cut into your profit margins
- × Potential increased tax because it will be classed as income
- × There may be a dip in the market, and the property won't have grown as you had anticipated, even after the refurb

BRRR – Buy, Refurbish, Refinance, Rent

What Is BRRR?

BRRR is a strategy where you buy a property, add value through refurbishment, then refinance it at a higher value, and finally rent it out. The goal is to pull most (or ideally all) of your initial investment back out while still holding the asset long-term.

How It Works?

You start by purchasing a property, typically one that's below market value and/or in need of improvement. Using cash or bridging finance, you complete the refurbishment to significantly increase its value. Once complete, you refinance onto a long-term mortgage based on the new, higher value, which allows you to repay the original finance and recycle your capital into your next deal.

Why BRRR?

BRRR is a powerful method for scaling your portfolio quickly, as it lets you reuse your money rather than locking it into one deal. You retain the asset, benefit from future capital growth and rental income, and have the ability to repeat the process again and again.

What Makes An Ideal BRRR Deal?

A rundown or unloved property that can be bought at a significant discount.

The potential to add substantial value through relatively low-cost refurbishments.

A strong end valuation to allow most of your funds to be pulled out.

Think: cosmetic upgrades, adding a bedroom, or converting unused space, not ground-up rebuilds or overly complex projects (unless you are more experienced).

Advantages

- ✓ Faster portfolio growth by recycling your capital
- ✓ Generates lump sums you can reinvest
- ✓ You keep the property and benefit from long-term rental income and capital appreciation
- ✓ Can significantly boost your return on investment (ROI)

Disadvantages & Risks

- × Renovation costs can spiral beyond budget or timeframe
- × Down valuations at the refinance stage can reduce how much money you can pull out
- × A market downturn could reduce the property's value or rental demand

- × Bridging finance can be costly if delays occur
- × Refurb can turn into a job if not systemised properly

Serviced Accommodation

What Is SA?

Renting the whole property (house or apartment) on a short-term basis, often by the night. There are 2 main types of customers, working people (contractors) or holiday makers.

How SA works?

You decorate and furnish the house, so it looks like a hotel, a home-from-home of sorts. The guests have everything on site that they would normally have at home. Guest often use an online platform to book their length of stay. The online travel agent (OTA) takes their % upon time of booking.

Why SA?

There is a lot of money to be made in the SA sector. A typical 2-bed property in our investment area that rents for £750pcm on an AST might achieve £75per night. You want your property to have an occupancy of 70-75%; much more means it's too cheap.

Ideal SA

In a town where there is a great all-year-round holiday trade, yet the market is not saturated. Or in a town with a lot of construction/regeneration taking place, and contractors will book your property for +3-month contracts. Having great transport connections is a big advantage if you are attracting the contractor's clientele.

Advantages

- ✓ You have much better cash flow when compared to a single BTL (if it's occupied)
- ✓ Possible tax efficiency if structured properly
- ✓ Since they are guests and not tenants, there is no AST, so you shouldn't need to evict anybody

Disadvantages & Risks

- × Your rent will fluctuate
- × Higher management fees
- × Higher operating costs
- × People may trash your property (same with any strategy other than flipping, really)
- × When using an online booking agent, they will take a good 15% of the money
- × You need to set up a system for the property to be regularly cleaned and maintained so that each guest feels well-kept

HMO

What Is An HMO?

House In Multiple Occupation. This is renting bedrooms out individually in a property rather than the whole house.

How HMOs Work?

You provide a communal area for the kitchen and dining room. Tenants then have their own space in their bedroom. You need to check that the property isn't in an Article 4 area, and you need to apply to your local authority for an HMO licence.

Why HMO?

It makes a house that would be on a single AST more profitable. With a single AST, your house is 100% occupied or 100% empty, i.e., it's an all-or-nothing situation. With HMOs, it's very rare that you have 0% occupancy; this means you should always have money coming into your account. A 3-bedroom house that would generate £1100pcm in our investment area if converted to a 4-bed mini HMO would generate £1600pcm, 5-bed £2000pcm. That's a lot more cash flow every month.

Ideal HMO

Like most of the other strategies, when you are acquiring the property, you want to get a great BMV deal. You will have carried out the refurb in line with your end user, i.e., blue collar, social housing, boutique, etc. You will have run your figures and made sure that your mortgage payment is paid, even if the property is 50% tenanted.

Advantages

- ✓ Higher levels of cash flow every month compared to BTL
- ✓ Risk is spread across multiple tenants
- ✓ Increased ROI compared to BTL

Disadvantages & Risks

- × You will need to find a specialist HMO letting agent who charges 12-15% of the rent
- × You need to deal with the council to ensure it meets regulations, etc
- × Higher regulation and licensing
- × Higher tenant turnover than BTLs. The build-out is dearer than a normal refurb since you have more requirements to meet, especially if you are fitting en-suites in every room

Deal Sourcing

What Is Deal Sourcing?

You find a property deal and sell that deal to an investor for a fee.

How Deal Sourcing Works?

You find a property, carry out necessary due diligence regarding the refurbishment costs, the ceiling price when the works are done, i.e., end value, and the possible monthly rental amount. You then package the deal for an investor and take a deal sourcing fee. The sourcing fee you charge should still make the deal attractive to the investor.

Why Deal Source?

Starting off with deal sourcing can provide you with experience in the property industry without having to have £££'s for deposits, etc. If you are looking at lots of deals a month, you may want to sell the other deals to somebody who wants to invest in them. If you charge £3k per deal and sell 1pcm, then it's £3000 towards your deposit for your own property investments.

Ideal Deal

A deal where the investor would have to be crazy not to invest, because even in a bad situation with an undervaluation, the deal still has great margins

Advantages

- ✓ Gain contacts
- ✓ Low entry fee
- ✓ Have lumps of cash to use towards your own portfolio
- ✓ It's scalable as a business model

Disadvantages & Risks

- × You need to make sure you are fully compliant
- × Your income could be very inconsistent
- × It's becoming a very saturated market, so you really need to stand out
- × You could just end up having another 'job'

Commercial Conversions

What Are Commercial Conversions?

Finding commercial premises and then converting them to residential property.

How Commercial Conversions Work?

Calculate if the property is a good candidate, i.e., refurbishment costs, end values per unit (GDV), and possible rental amounts. Close to amenities. Seek planning permission.

Why Commercial Conversions?

There are many commercial properties up and down the country that are empty. These properties can be purchased at the BMV, where a lower SDLT is payable, and converted to residential homes. They can be converted into self-contained units, HMOs, or a combination. The figures are normally much more than a standard residential sale, but the upside is much greater, too.

Advantages

- ✓ Massive chance to add significant value
- ✓ Many commercial-residential can be done under PD
- ✓ Higher profit margins
- ✓ Potential for multiple units

Disadvantages & Risks

- × High capital requirement
- × Finding the unit and getting planning permission

- × Much dearer build-out costs
- × Longer build-out time
- × Uncertain end values (GDV)

Assisted Sales

What Are Assisted Sales?

You find a property that has been on the market for a long time and has not had any offers. You can see that with a refurbishment, you will comfortably be able to sell the property. You agree with the vendor to carry out the work and have a % of the uplift in purchase price.

How Assisted Sales Work?

You carry out the refurbishment to add value. This should help speed up the time it takes to agree on a sale. The sale should be at a higher price than pre-refurbishment.

Why Assisted Sales?

A vendor may do this because they realise their house has not sold. You are taking on some of the risk, and they have an increased chance of securing a sale.

Advantages

- ✓ You don't have to come up with the 25% deposit
- ✓ You don't need to pay the 5% SDLT

- ✓ Work can be carried out with the vendors still in the property, which can substantially reduce holding costs

Disadvantages & Risks

If the agreement is not secure, you may have the rug pulled from underneath you, i.e., they sell the property and give you nothing.

Title Splits

What Are Title Splits?

Purchasing a freehold property, often a MUFB (multi-unit freehold block), and splitting the title into separate leases. Selling or raising finance against each lease

How Title Splits Work?

Speak to a solicitor competent in title splits and explain your plans.

Why Title Splits?

Breaking properties down and selling them as parts is worth more than selling them as a whole.

Advantages

- ✓ Uplift in value without having to do any refurbishment
- ✓ You can choose to sell all the units, keep some, or keep all of them, i.e, multiple exit strategies

Disadvantages & Risks

- × Can be complex, so you must use a specialist solicitor with a proven track record
- × Some lenders are stricter on their requirements

Some strategies can be combined with creative financing methods like Rent to Rent, Lease Options, or Exchange with Delayed Completion. We cover these in detail in the creative financing section of the book.

In Summary

Many investors specialise in 1 strategy but also diversify their portfolio by using other strategies too. My advice would be to have a broad strokes knowledge of the different strategies, but aim to master 1 before moving on to the next. Once you are extremely confident in 1 strategy, then concentrate on another and become a master in that too. Do not bounce from 1 strategy to another because the grass always appears to be greener. You need to gain experience and competence before you move on to the next.

Chapter 19

How To Choose The Right Strategy For Your Goals?

Your property strategy must be a reflection of your unique goals, resources, and risk appetite. Clarity on your "why" turns overwhelming choices into confident action. Master one path, avoid shiny distractions, and build a business that lasts, not a quick fix that fades.

The right property strategy depends entirely on your goals, so before anything else, you need to get clear on your *why*.

Are you looking to:

- Escape the 9–5 and replace your income?
- Build out a nice passive income stream (or multiple streams)?
- Build long-term wealth for your future while still enjoying your current job?
- Make sure your business profits are working harder than sitting in a bank earning 0% interest.

Once you know *why* you're doing this, choosing the right strategy becomes a lot easier.

What's Right For You?

A lot of our mentees are looking for increased cash flow, while others are focused on capital growth. If that sounds like you, then something like BRRR could be a great fit.

But remember; every strategy has its own pros and cons. Your risk tolerance, your resources, and your time availability should all influence your decision.

- Got a high risk tolerance and good experience? You might be drawn to commercial to residential conversions
- Want to play it steady and safe? A traditional BTL is still a solid strategy
- Short on cash but willing to hustle? Rent-to-Rent could be your entry point
- Got capital but no time? You might want to consider joint ventures

Be Wary Of "Shiny Penny Syndrome"

Once you start immersing yourself in the property world, you'll see people claiming:

"I made £1,000,000 in 6 weeks" or "Become financially free in 90 days with just ONE deal."

Now, I'm not saying these things never happen, but they're the exception, not the rule.

I'm not here to sell you a dream. In the **Black Belt Property Academy,** we don't sell courses; we are here to help you build a portfolio that works long-term and to transform your knowledge and mindset.

The people who succeed in this game don't bounce between every strategy. They master one, build consistency, and *then* they evolve. You might start with BTL, then move to HMO, and eventually go into commercial conversions. But not all at once.

Think In Phases

Here's A Possible Journey:

- Start with 1 BTL to build knowledge and experience (year 1)
- Progress to 2 BTLs - BRRR's for higher returns (year 2)
- Use that income to fund your first HMO project for higher cash flow (year 3)
- Recycle your capital and do multiple BRRRs (year 4)
- Once your portfolio is solid, scale up to commercial to residential projects and aim to do
- 1-2 flips per year for lumps of cash (year 5)

There is no right or wrong way; the main thing is that you start. One of the worst things you can do is read this book and think '*that's great – I'm going to start on Monday*' then never do anything because life gets in the way. Before you start anything, ask yourself: *"What's my exit plan?"*Am I keeping for wealth, or flipping for cash?

Plans will change, and that's OK, but having a plan beats winging it every time.

In Summary

Your property strategy should reflect your current resources, risk tolerance, and long-term goals. Whether you're seeking cash flow, capital growth, or creative ways to get started with little capital, there is a strategy that fits, but only if you're clear on your "*why*." Focus on mastering one strategy before moving on to the next, and avoid being distracted by the hype of overnight success stories. Black Belts aren't built overnight; it takes time. Know what you're working with: do you have time, money, or a strong network? Are you building long-term wealth or looking to create short-term income? Map out your game plan early, even if it evolves, and make sure each move you make supports your bigger picture. Clarity beats complexity every time.

Chapter 20

The Right Deals And The Ones To Avoid

Success in property investing comes from disciplined buying based on clear goals, market knowledge, and strict price control, not chasing hype or emotion.

We have a clear, systemised formula for what to buy and what not to buy. However, knowing our investment area very well and understanding current demands often means we don't need to rely solely on a formula. For example, if an agent calls about a property in a particular area listed at £140,000, we usually know the rent within £25 per calendar month, the type of tenant it will attract, and whether it's a good deal or not. Just a heads up, agents don't usually call when the market is going up; they tend to forget your number until they need to meet sales targets.

Being educated and clear about your strategy will determine your purchasing criteria. If we focused solely on flips, we'd look for three-bedroom semi-detached houses or larger in good to great areas. If our plan was to buy properties to lease to social housing providers on a five-year contract, we'd target two-bedroom homes in 'low to mid-tier' areas—somewhere rated about 3 on a scale from 1 to 10, where 10 is the most premium. For HMOs, proximity to main roads, shops, and excellent transport links is essential.

Don't just listen to what a mate once told you. Work out what you want to achieve from property investing and then work backwards. Be wary of agents telling you things like *"It's a great buy, the yield is over 10%."* They are almost always referring to gross yield, which doesn't account for all costs. Instead, you need to know how much you can pull out of the deal and your Return on Capital Employed (ROCE) to decide if a deal is worth pursuing.

To avoid rental headaches, keep these in mind: properties should be near shops (but not a strip of endless takeaways and pound shops), close to transport links like bus routes, trams, or trains, near large employers, and not located in the worst parts of town. Our best rentals are near convenience stores, right on or close to A-roads, and within a short walk or drive of major transport hubs. Few people want to rent a house in the sticks.' While it's not impossible to find tenants there, narrowing your pool of tenants will mean longer void periods.

Our Buy-To-Let Criteria

For our standard buy-to-lets, we look in average areas where tenants typically have little or no aspiration to become homeowners. Like most investors, we want tenants who move in, pay rent on time, look after the property, and stay long-term. We aim to lock in profit from day one by securing properties as low as possible. For example, a recent two-bedroom buy-to-let was listed for £150,000, but we purchased it for £110,000—a 36% discount. We used the BRRR (Buy, Refurbish, Rent, Refinance) strategy and managed to pull most of our money back out; we ended up leaving approx £6k in the deal.

We don't just want to park our money somewhere; we want properties where we can add value. That's why we prefer homes that need refurbishment, especially back-to-brick refurbishments, which fit well with the BRRR approach.

When We Bend The Rules?

Occasionally, if a property is priced really well and can be leased to a social housing provider for five years with reasonable cash flow, we will consider it, even if it doesn't meet all our usual criteria.

Who Do We Rent To?

Finding tenants isn't just about them having a pulse and money—though in 2007, I made that mistake by letting anyone who could pay rent move in without proper checks. Looking back, it was a big error, but at least I took action and learned from those mistakes. Even if a tenant meets all criteria, if you have a gut feeling something's off, trust it. It's better to leave a property empty a little longer and wait for the right tenant than accept trouble.

A good managing agent should conduct the following essential checks: verify the tenant's legal right to rent in the UK, confirm their income to ensure they can afford the rent, run credit checks for any County Court Judgments (CCJs) or bankruptcies, obtain references from previous landlords, and process standard application forms, including guarantor checks if necessary.

Our personal criteria are even stricter: tenants must have rental experience with a history of on-time payments. If an agent tells us, *"They pay, but sometimes it's late, but they always catch up,"* we decline. We'd rather the property stay empty than take on a problematic tenant. We prefer working tenants, ideally with both parents employed, and we don't rent to two friends (for example, two men or two women sharing) who can't realistically afford to live alone. Typically, one party moves out and the other struggles to pay the rent, causing problems.

While we are not against non-working tenants, we aim to reduce risk by renting to working tenants. When rent was paid directly from councils to us, non-working tenants were less risky. But once the rent went to the tenants' accounts first, late, and partial payments increased. You may also want to consider a social media check or even a tenant interview. After all, it's your property and you're taking the risk, so you can be as thorough as you want.

Remember, you are running a business and should do everything you can to stack the odds in your favour.

Flips

With flips, smaller houses usually mean smaller profits, unless you've secured an exceptional deal. We have never invested in apartments because they are harder to increase in value compared to two or three-bedroom houses. For example, if you have a three-bedroom semi and can add an extra bedroom or additional living space through permitted development, you could make a profit of £30'000- £40'000 or more. Success with flips comes down to buying at the right price, selecting the right location, sticking to your refurbishment budget, knowing your end user, and ensuring a quality finish.

Don't expect to buy in a poor area, split a large bedroom into two small rooms by putting up a stud wall, and make a £30'000 profit.

What We Don't Buy?

We avoid expensive properties. It might seem obvious, but emotions often cloud judgment. Don't get into bidding wars just because you 'must' have a property. Always base your maximum price on solid calculations and never go above it. Develop that Black Belt Discipline.

We don't buy off-plan properties. The early 2000s saw a boom in off-plan investments, but I've always been skeptical because there's a risk the builder might go bust. New builds also come at a premium price, and the money tied up during construction means you miss out on rental income for 12–18 months. Off-plan doesn't fit our strategy.

We don't buy abroad. While it might seem appealing, owning property overseas can be a headache; language barriers, legal differences, currency risk, and the logistics of managing a property from afar through a different language all add complexity. I prefer renting a holiday home when abroad rather than owning one.

We avoid scattergun approaches where properties are bought all over the country. This can make managing them difficult and prevent building good relationships with local agents, managing companies, and tradespeople. All our properties are within the same area to keep things manageable and efficient. However, buying properties all over the country can be a good idea, and it can force you to be 100% hands-off.

We don't buy new builds because they are generally more expensive and offer little chance to add value. Many new builds are designed with "hidden" compromises like smaller rooms or less durable fixtures. We prefer properties at least 20 years old where we can add value through renovations.

What You Should Buy?

Some investors shy away from rundown properties, but these are a key part of the BRRR strategy. There's a difference between a property that is rundown but habitable and one that's uninhabitable or has serious structural issues. We avoid properties with big problems like leaning gable ends or major foundation issues. We prefer quotes over estimates to know exactly how much refurbishments will cost.

Each property must cash flow from the day a tenant moves in, with a baseline of at least £300 per calendar month profit for a single BTL, and £600pcm for a 4-5 bed HMO.

Location is important; your property should be close to amenities such as hospitals, transport links, corner shops, parks, and schools, depending on your target tenant. Our tenants are usually small families, so proximity to primary schools and shops matters.

You also need a steady supply of tenants. Buying the same style of property, doing similar refurbishments, and attracting the same tenant type makes managing your portfolio simpler.

Properties should be local to each other to maximize efficiency and build strong relationships with local agents and tradespeople.

We always aim to lock in profit from day one. Here are some recent deals we have completed to illustrate this point:

- A property listed at £130'000 was agreed at £111'000 (minor £4,000 refurb, 15% BMV)
- Another at £150' 000 we purchased for £110'000 (27% BMV).
- Another listed at £145'000 we purchased for £105'000 (27% BMV)

- Another listed at £99'000 (sold as seen) we purchased for £75'000 (24% BMV)

You make money when you buy, not when you sell.

Choosing The Right Neighbourhood

We avoid the very worst neighbourhoods despite their low prices and high yields. The challenges; like difficulty collecting rent, longer vacancy periods, and limited capital growth, outweigh the benefits.

On the flip side, we don't buy in the most expensive and prestigious areas either. We target neighbourhoods ranked around 4 to 6 on a 1-to-10 scale, where 1 is the worst and 10 is the best. These areas offer the best balance of cash flow and capital growth.

Becoming deeply familiar with your chosen area is critical. Knowing subareas and local dynamics helps you make smarter purchases and build strong connections with agents and tradespeople.

In Summary

A good deal is one that makes money, but what counts as "*good*" depends on your goals. If you want a reliable monthly cash flow, a standard buy-to-let in a reasonably priced area may not meet all your needs. For long-term wealth through capital growth, a two- or three-bedroom terrace requiring minimal work can be ideal.

The key is to know your criteria and stick to them. For buy-and-hold investors, even properties that aren't wrecks can steadily build wealth over time. Buying well, understanding your market, and focusing on value and location will set you up for success.

Chapter 21
Multiple Streams Of Property Income

Wealthy investors don't rely on one income stream; they build multiple, layered property incomes that work together to create freedom, flexibility, and long-term wealth.

Most people think there are only one or two ways to make money in property. You either buy a house to rent it out, or you buy a house, renovate it, and sell it for a profit. That's what the average person believes, but if you're serious about becoming a professional investor, you must understand that there are multiple income streams within property, and learning to stack them is how true wealth is built.

The great thing about property is that it's all part of the same ecosystem. As your knowledge and experience grow in one area, it naturally spills over into others. Over time, your ability to spot opportunities increases, and your skillset expands. Before long, you're earning from more than one stream, sometimes from the same property.

Below are the main ways property investors generate income, both active and passive, and how you can do the same.

Monthly Rental Income

This is one of the most popular and well-known strategies, and for good reason. You purchase a property, rent it out for more than your finance and operational costs, and keep the surplus as monthly cash flow. When done properly, it's passive income. If you've bought well, completed a smart refurb, and have solid systems in place, you'll get paid every month whether you're working or not. I love this side of property, and it's the main reason I got into it back in 2007.

Building reliable cash flow is the foundation of financial independence. Long-term wealth comes from assets that pay you over and over again, not just once.

Flipping For Profit

Flipping is simple in theory: buy low, sell high. It's an excellent way to generate lump sums of cash, especially early in your investing journey. You might find a discounted property and resell it without even doing a refurb, or you might add value through renovations and then sell on the open market.

The issue with flipping is that it's transactional. Once the deal is done, the income stops. That's why it's best used to fund long-term portfolio growth, not as your main strategy.

Unlocking Equity (Through Time Or BRRR)

Over time, property tends to go up in value, and if you hold assets long enough, you can benefit from that appreciation. The smarter move is to force that appreciation through refurbishment and then refinance. This allows you to release equity (tax-free because it's debt) and reinvest it into more deals.

This is the power behind the BRRR strategy: buy, refurb, refinance, and rent out. You get the capital back to go again, while holding an income-producing asset that someone else is paying off for you.

Rent-To-Rent

This is a powerful strategy that allows you to generate monthly income without owning the property. You take control of a property under a management agreement or lease, pay the landlord a fixed amount each month, and then rent the property out at a higher rate.

For example, you might pay a landlord £500 per month, but earn £1,000 using it as a Serviced Accommodation (SA) unit, or £1,200 as an HMO. The landlord accepts a slightly lower rent because it's guaranteed, and you earn the difference. This strategy works particularly well when applied to HMOs or SAs in high-demand areas.

There will be some upfront costs to get the property in the right condition, but if you've done your due diligence properly, you'll recoup those quickly and start cash flowing soon after.

Purchase Lease Options (PLOs)

With a purchase lease option, you gain control of a property without needing the full 25% deposit upfront. You benefit from the monthly cash flow during the lease period and then purchase the property at an agreed price later, ideally below market value.

If you've chosen the right property and the market moves in your favour, you lock in equity at the end of the term. It's a smart way to gain control now, profit monthly, and benefit from future appreciation.

Deal Sourcing

Deal sourcing is the art of finding great investment opportunities and selling them on to other investors for a fee. You act as the middleman/woman, connecting motivated sellers with serious buyers. In return, you earn a sourcing fee, often between £2'000 and £5'000 per deal (or more depending on the value of the property).

Investors will expect clear data: the expected GDV, estimated refurb costs, rental projections, and return on capital employed (ROCE). This is a great strategy to build cash reserves and learn how to stack deals, especially if you're not ready to buy property yourself just yet.

You'll need to become compliant (register with HMRC for Anti Money Laundering (AML), have Public Indemnity (PI) insurance, etc.), but once that's in place, it can become a reliable cash generator.

Property Management

If you already manage your own portfolio, you can offer that same service to other investors. Property management companies typically charge around 10% of monthly rent, and while it is a job (you're trading time for money), it's a great way to build recurring income, grow your knowledge of the lettings market, and build out your power team.

The first few properties are the most time-consuming while systems are put in place, but after that, management becomes much more efficient. The more units you manage, the more economies of scale kick in, and eventually, you can outsource the day-to-day operations and keep the margin.

Adding Value Through Planning Or Development

Advanced investors often look to create value through planning gains, conversions, or new builds. This might include turning a single-family home into a 6-bed HMO, splitting one property into two flats, or adding a small extension to increase the footprint and value. As you become more experienced, you start to ask '*what could I do with this property*' – you will see far past the normal rental options.

These projects typically require more experience (or a strong professional team), but the profits can be substantial. Development is where serious equity is made, but only when done with precision and proper planning.

Black Belt Insight

Most amateur investors focus on one or two streams, usually rental income and long-term appreciation. Initially, there is nothing wrong with that. Professionals know better, and they stack income layers. They extract cash flow, refinance equity, source deals, and sometimes even manage other people's properties, all from the same base of knowledge and infrastructure.

This is how long-term wealth is built in property, not by doing one thing, but by learning how to build systems that pay you in multiple ways, often from the same deal.

In Summary

Wealthy investors don't rely on a single income stream. They build portfolios that combine cash flow, capital growth, refinancing, deal sourcing, and recurring income; all working together. Even if you're starting with little or no capital, you can learn the ropes through rent-to-rent, deal sourcing, or management services, and use the income to fund your first property purchase. From there, you can begin stacking income streams and scaling your portfolio. It will take time, but not a lifetime. Start where you are and focus on learning. Stack the strategies as your skills grow. Build a property business that pays you, not one that depends on you.

********* APPLICATION NOTICE *********

Ready To Become A Black Belt Investor?

This is not for everyone.

The Black Belt Property Academy exists for investors who are ready to think, act, and grow with discipline. Not for those chasing shortcuts.

Here, membership is earned. Progress is deliberate. Execution, feedback, and standards matter more than information or tactics.

Inside the Academy, you will:

- ✓ Apply a proven, step-by-step system for building property portfolios
- ✓ Develop the judgement and discipline that separates serious investors from dabblers
- ✓ Learn to navigate risk calmly and professionally
- ✓ Move forward with structure, clarity, and accountability

Entry is by application only. Spaces are deliberately limited. Not everyone will qualify and that is the point.

If this resonates, take the next step. Scan the QR code or visit **DervishDervish.com** to apply for the next Accelerator.

Membership begins when readiness meets opportunity.

********* APPLICATION NOTICE *********

PART 4

Finding, Funding & Analysing Deals

Getting the right funding is essential, but knowing how to spot and secure a great deal is just as important. In this section, you'll explore both traditional and creative finance strategies, from mortgages and bridging loans to lease options and delayed completions. You'll also learn how to analyse deals with confidence, work effectively with estate agents, and view properties like a professional investor. The goal is simple: help you fund smarter, buy better, and move forward with clarity.

Chapter 22

Working With Estate Agents Like A Professional Investor

Estate agents are key partners in your investment journey. Build genuine relationships, stay consistent, verify details, and keep in touch. This turns agents into trusted allies who help you find the best deals and manage your properties smoothly.

If you are just starting out in your property investing journey, it's very likely you will get your deals from estate agents. Deal sourcers are good, but there is nothing wrong with buying through agents if you have worked out the numbers and the deal still works. Getting direct to vendor (D2V) deals will always be the best deals, but you need to have a systemised process and then work the system. D2V is not just about posting 20 letters sporadically and then gaining a fantastic deal. D2V, like everything, needs work. D2V marketing is not a 1-off event; it's a repeatable system.

Estate agents often get a bit of a bad rap. From the outside looking in, it's quite easy to understand why some people think they charge ever-increasing fees for not really doing that much. Fees for sale can be anything from 1% sale price up to £5k, this is why many people at 1 point went with Purple Bricks, who charged a fraction of what high street agents charge (but also offered a fraction of the service). However, just as with any industry, there are good ones and bad ones. I have worked with some great agents over the years, both in sales and on the rental side of things. I have also had the 'pleasure' of working with bad ones, too. The more experienced you become, the quicker you will be able to spot great agents from mediocre/bad ones.

You are likely to deal with agents.

- Building relationships and letting them know what you do
- Pre-sale = Viewing properties
- Sale agreed = Purchasing a property
- Refurb done and ready for tenants = Managing 1 of your properties

How Do You Know If They Are Good?

At the Academy, we suggest that mentees make contact with them, go in, or telephone. I prefer to go in so I can actually see who I'm dealing with, but obviously, if you are investing far away from your home, then it's going to be much easier to telephone them. Things I would be looking out for:

- Are they stand-off-ish?
- Do they look at you as if you are interrupting their day?
- Does their shop present well? If it's disorganised, imagine what their business practices must be like
- Do you get the sense they will roll their eyes as soon as you have gone?
- Can they give you accurate information?

Regarding accurate information, you should have thoroughly researched the area so you know just as much as they do in terms of what the demand for rentals of your type is, what the price range is, and how long they stay on the market. If an agent says that they can achieve significantly more pcm than the average, then be aware, likewise if they say the property will let immediately, but your research says they take 4 weeks to let. Again, this all circles back to you knowing your investment area, knowing your numbers, and your important metrics. Every deal you look at, you need to have done ample due diligence.

The Squeaky Wheel Gets The Oil

Continually remind agents that you are investing. If you manage to purchase a property through an agent, then clearly let them know you are after more, and this was not just a 1-off thing. If you build up relationships with agents, then you start to get into their 'inner circle'. You want them to think of you if a particular property becomes available that meets your criteria. Buying 1 property from them is great, but don't think that they will remember you when the next deal comes along. They spend their days selling properties, so although it's a big day for you picking up the keys, it's just another day for them. You must touch base with the agents regularly, through viewings, emails, drop-ins, physical letters, etc.

If you only have a connection and rapport with 1 agent in 1 agency and that person changes shop or even worse, changes careers, then you're back to square 1. Continually build out your network. We all know that we need to network, network, network, but that is not just for brand awareness or raising private finance; it's to build up your power team, too. I would suggest you have a list of estate agents within your investment area and create a schedule that tells you which agents you are visiting and when. Depending on your availability, I would plan to visit them every 4 weeks, 6 weeks at the maximum. Variety in your business practice is bad, though, so make sure it's every 4, 5, or 6 weeks, not 2 weeks, then 8 weeks later, then 3 weeks after that. Creating and following your systems will result in anticipated deal flow. The more systemised you make your operations, the more your business benefits.

Cookies

Some people suggest taking in cookies and coffee, etc, to break the ice. I'm not a fan of this approach, although some fellow investors swear by it. For me, it would feel a bit too false. I prefer to handwrite them a thank-you letter following our first connection and then follow up 2-3 weeks later. I want them to know my face and know that I'm still actively investing. If you feel comfortable taking in some cookies or a cake, then go for it – anything that will bring you front and centre in their minds.

Business Cards

I would not underestimate this old practice. Some of my mentees spend hours pondering over a design, or just go for the electronic ones. Yes, the design should look professional, but remember it should only contain crucial information: your picture, your phone number, your email, and what you do. I always recommend physical business cards because you are giving them something tangible, as opposed to another link they open on their already overwhelmed browser. You must have a picture of yourself on the card so the agent can put a face to the name. If you give out your business card, make sure you collect one in return and then schedule a follow-up.

You can put them on your contact list and make sure they hear from you regularly.

Never Assume: Always Verify

The *'never assume, always verify'* concept can be applied to so many areas of your business, life, and property investing. Being specific to estate agents, here are things I would never assume and would always want clarity on

- *"Has my property been listed yet?"*
    - They may have said that the property will be live within 24 hours of taking the pictures, but always verify.
- *"Have we had any applicants yet?"*
    - Once it's online, I would check within 3 days how many applicants it has had, I would then check on day 7, and then again on day 11. If it's quiet, then you may have overpriced the property, or the agent didn't do a compelling listing. December is a notorious time to try and find a tenant, so don't reduce your price too much if it's during the 15th-31st December.
- *"You do pre-check applicants before doing viewings, don't you?"*
    - One agent we worked with just offered a block viewing for anybody with a pulse. You don't want this. You want 'qualified' people to view the property only, not people who like it but have no way of affording it. The agent may feed back to you that they had 10 people turn up (failing to tell you it's really 5 couples) and then state they had no applications. This then might lead you to reduce the price.

If you have done your correct DD and priced it properly, then it will go.

- *"You are clear on who I want and, more importantly, who I don't want in the property?"*
    - Confirm this to them at least two times; you don't want them to tell you that they have a great applicant, but it goes against what you wanted. We had 2 gentlemen move into 1 of our properties, and the agent made it out that they were a couple. It transpired that they had both split up from their partners, and our house was a stepping stone for both. They were in for 6 months only. You don't want this. You want long-term tenants.
- *"What happens if you find a tenant, they pay the necessary fees, but then change their mind? Do we need to pay for you to find another tenant again?"*
    - Check with your agent that their fees are only paid once the tenant has paid everything. The more the tenant pays, the stronger they are.

Person-2-Person (Not B2B)

I'm a firm believer that it's not B2B or B2C but P2P. If you want to be in property for the long run, then it's in your best interests to build relationships; after all, it's not what you know but who knows you. Build relationships with multiple agents so that you are casting a big net. People do business with people they like, find out the culture of the agency and its team, and if it aligns with your goals, then build on the relationship. It took me a while to understand that building relationships is a high-value task.

The success of your portfolio and ultimately your business is down to how many people know and like you.

Bad Experience With Agents

Being in business for over 20 years and building a very successful Karate school, I was continually training my team on positive and negative touch points. Any interaction a lead, enquiry, family, parent, or student has with our school was either a positive or negative touch point. We are always adding to or withdrawing from their emotional bank account. If you are looking to 1 day bring in-house your own properties for management then remember that first impressions count and that every interaction they have with you will either be a deposit or withdrawal from their personal account. Here are just a few things that have rubbed me the wrong way

- They said they will let you know when a certain property becomes available, and then you find out it's gone to another investor for a fantastic price. Take ownership, though. This is our fault because we did not pester them enough, or the other investor had a stronger rapport with the agent
- They gradually increase their fees because they feel you won't check or shift your business to another agent
- Not appreciating your time and constantly being late for viewings
- Only calling you when they are struggling to meet targets
- Sending out a trade to replace a light bulb, which costs you £75, because the tenant didn't know how to

- Asking you to manage your property even though that's what they are paid for, i.e., they send emails saying 'do you want to arrange with your contractor or should we arrange it'

Make sure that if a letting agent is managing your property, they are actually carrying out regular inspections. The rent coming in on time every time should be standard procedure, but a few agents think that if the rent is coming in on time every time, then why does the landlord need to know about the state of the property? To some extent, I can see this, but we have had tenants that don't tell you if the kitchen ceiling has fallen down or the boiler is leaking, the shower is leaking into the downstairs kitchen, they can't lock the back door, plus much more. Reading between the lines, I think this may have been because the landlord they previously dealt with may have seen it as the tenant's fault, which possibly led to giving them notice. We have our own systems that tell us when a property is due for an inspection. We then politely nudge the agent to ask when this is scheduled to be carried out (trust but always verify).

Why Do We Want Regular Inspections?

For us, it's so that we can try to prevent any maintenance issue from getting worse, I don't know any maintenance issue that manages to fix itself. Having regular inspections also allows us to see how the tenant is looking after the property, i.e, are they letting the property breathe. Kitchens and bathrooms are often where we have most problems, and it's often because of poor ventilation. Yes, tenants are provided with a 'how to rent' leaflet upon first signing the agreement, but how many of them actually read it thoroughly and then do exactly what it says?

We have a very keen agent who does inspections every 3 months, which is great. We have others who do them every 6 months, and 1 agent who only did it in month 9 of a 12-month AST. For us, the 9-month mark is way too long; the 6-month one for a new tenant, I believe, is also too long. I think the best inspections are month 3, month 6, and if it's all well, then maybe every 6 months, but make sure the tenants know to report any issue so you can deal with it.

How To Make Your Offer Stand Out And Get Accepted?

Agents will work with dozens of buyers every week. So how do you stand out and increase the chances your offer is chosen – especially if your offer isn't the highest? You need to come across as very professional and the complete opposite of a time waster. For new agents that we make offers with, we send an email early in the morning the day after the viewing. The email is from our official email address, i.e. not a '@hotmail' account, the email has a branded letter head which includes our offer subject to survey. The email also contains the following:

- Our DIP (Decision In Principle)
- Bank statement showing proof of funds (if we have not worked with this agent previously)
- Email address and physical address of the solicitors we use
- An email from our broker saying he can raise finance through several ways
- Contact details for another agent who can confirm we do not mess people around

You want the agent to think '*these guys are serious*'. In doing so, when they contact the vendor, they should be able to suggest which offer they take. Again, this links back to a motivated seller – if yours is a lower offer, but you are 100% ready to go, and the agent knows you will follow through, then the vendor should take your guidance. It doesn't always work, but you want to present yourself as professional.

In Summary

If you are not doing any direct vendor marketing or dealing with a deal sourcer, then chances are that estate agents are going to be 100% your main source of deals. Likewise, if you are not managing your properties yourself, which I would always avoid, you need to work with the best agents. You therefore need to befriend them so that you are in with a good chance of getting decent properties at reasonable prices.

Chapter 23
Finding And Working With Motivated Sellers

Your best property deals will always come from motivation, not negotiation. When you understand why someone is selling, you unlock the price no one else can.

If you want to scale your property portfolio and create great monthly cash flow, then finding motivated sellers is crucial to your growth and success. You will find it very difficult to secure any great deals from sellers who are not motivated to sell in the first place.

When we first started out back in 2007, we used to view properties and put in offers, hoping somebody would bite. In fact, I lied, the first 3 properties we bought, we did no negotiation whatsoever, we paid the full asking price (what an amateur) when we started to put in '*low-ball*' offers, which should be classed as '*realistic*' offers, 9 out of 10 of these were rejected immediately. As time went on and as I educated myself more, I realised the offers that were accepted were often because the seller was motivated to sell. Our best deals over the past 10 years have been from motivated sellers.

If you have a look at one of the online property portals, you may find that some properties have been on for 9 months or more. At the time of writing this, I can think of 3 properties that have been on for over a year, and the price is exactly the same. There are, of course, many reasons for this. Common reasons are that it might be priced way too high, the vendor cannot afford to sell it any cheaper, or they were just testing the market and wanted to see if they could sell it. However, with motivated sellers, they need to sell because the property is causing them too much of a problem (financial or emotional, or both). Motivated sellers tend to drop the price every few weeks because time is against them. If you notice a property seems to be being reduced quite regularly, every 4 weeks or so, then that's a sign they are motivated to sell. It might not mean they are in financial difficulty, but they might have had an offer accepted on another house and need to sell theirs to move on.

If the property is for sale at an unrealistically high price, then this might be down to the agent who advised it was worth that 'inflated' amount just to secure the deal. Then, after they have secured the listing, they leave it on the market for a while, then, due to lack of interest, viewings, and offers, reduce the price to a more competitive price (this price is often what the other agents initially valued it at). It's not nice, but it does happen. When you start to know more and learn more about your investment area, you will notice which agents tend to list the highest.

There are many reasons why people will want to sell their property below its true value.

- They may be struggling to make the mortgage payments (due to a financial situation or because they have moved in with a partner and now have 2 houses)
- They have no equity to cover the selling fees (estate agents and solicitors), which means it will cost them to sell the property

- They have to sell it because they are facing bankruptcy and need cash
- They are now divorced or getting divorced, and it was their family home
- They have lost their job or had a reduction in pay
- They are suffering a downturn in their own business
- They are emigrating
- It needs a lot of work and spending on it to bring it up to standard, and they don't have the money, time, or experience
- The interest rate has now increased, and they can't keep up the payments (this happened in 2021 when interest rates increased)
- It has bad memories, and they just want to get rid of it asap

These are just some of the reasons, but ultimately, whatever the reason is, it's making them motivated to sell.

Not Everybody Thinks Like You

As an investor, you might think, why don't they keep the property and make some money from it. Possible reasons might be:

- They might not want to rent it themselves, dealing with everything that goes with tenancies
- They may not be able to find a suitable tenant for it
- They have done that before and had a bad experience
- The property has too many bad memories, etc

If the vendor needs the money quickly and time is crucial, then they are often willing to sell the property at BMV to get it over the line quicker; they don't have time or can't afford to have it on the market for months. They value the security that an agreed sale offers.

If the vendor has accrued lots of debt and it keeps building, then they will be more motivated to sell at a lower price.

As you become more experienced, you will be able to spot the signs of motivated and unmotivated sellers. If you are doing all your viewings through estate agents, then it's best practice to say you are only available in the evenings and weekends, i.e., when the agent isn't available for viewings. You will then get to speak to the vendor, and hopefully, you can find out more about why they are selling. If you use the online-only agents where vendors do the viewings themselves, this is a great way to speak directly to the vendor. Unfortunately, it's not likely you will be able to do this with vacant properties, but if you get to meet the vendor directly, then fantastic, they might be a tired landlord and looking to offload some/all their stock, what a perfect opportunity this is. We have secured a few properties at great prices by doing this. We didn't cut out the agent, but from building rapport on the viewing, we secured a great deal for both parties. It always needs to be a win-win scenario.

How Do You Find Motivated Sellers?

Market your services. The more people who know you buy properties and can act quickly, the more people should be contacting you. We are all familiar with the saying '*it's not what you know, it's who you know*', but in the business world, that is modified to '*it's not who you know, it's who knows you*'.

Direct marketing works; sending letters or postcards to properties that look distressed will get you leads. This book is not about how to design and systemise direct marketing campaigns, but it's important to know that sending 50 letters out is not likely to get you leads. Sending 50 letters to the same houses every 6 weeks for several months will generate leads.

It's a cliché answer, but network. The more you network, the more leads and deals you will get.

In Summary

You can waste so much time viewing properties where the sellers aren't motivated to sell. Finding motivated sellers is a proven way to secure a great deal. When you do get to meet the vendors, try to subtly find out why they are moving on. The more background information you have, the better your chances of securing a great deal.

Chapter 24

How Professional Investors Assess Properties?

Viewings aren't just inspections; they're your chance to spot real deals, build key relationships, and sharpen your investment skills. Show up ready, focus on the numbers, and treat every viewing as a step toward success.

This is the part of your property investing journey where the rubber meets the road. The viewings you attend are when you can confirm that your initial refurbishment calculations done during your research phase are correct or incorrect. I would suggest you only book viewings on properties that you have already done refurb costs for, and that appear to be a deal.

When you are looking to purchase your first investment property, going on a viewing may be a bit daunting, especially if you have never done one before. Some of my mentees said they felt like they had '*imposter syndrome*'. They felt that the agent was looking at them, thinking '*you're new to this…you don't know what you're doing*' – again, negative thoughts were creeping in. You must have self-belief that you are going to be successful at property investing, and by attending viewings, you are on that journey. By reading this book, you have shown that you are already very committed to becoming a better, more professional property investor. Regardless, going on viewings is a must if you are going to be a hands-on investor (or at least hands-on during the acquisition phase).

What To Look For On Property Viewings?

There are many things as an investor that you should be looking for at viewings. The structural side of things is the same as if you were buying your own home, but for an investment, there are different criteria.

It's useful to mention here that a viewing should be looked at as a 1:1 meeting with an agent, or if you are lucky, the vendor, so prepare questions ahead of time. For the agent, ask them questions about other similar properties, any sales that have fallen through, etc. If you are meeting with the vendor, gently ask about the area (even if you know the area well) and try to find out why they are moving, whether it is because of their job, downsizing, upsizing, or separation. Always compliment them on the house and never criticize the furniture or decoration.

Before Booking A Viewing

Numbers

Before you even book a viewing, though, make sure you have run your numbers to check that the deal stacks. We do not waste time attending viewings where the deal does not even stack. Don't be a 'tyre kicker', you don't want that reputation from estate agents. Now, only book in viewings where the deal stacks can limit the potential properties you have to view. However, if you are a complete beginner, then I would be a bit more flexible with your criteria. Let me clarify, though, that I'm only saying to be flexible when booking the viewings, do not be flexible on your criteria for calculating if the deal works or not. Never fudge the numbers just so you can say you have acquired a property. One of the worst things you can do is to invest in a property just to stroke your ego – keep emotion out of it and base it solely on the numbers.

Viewing Report/Checklist

If you want access to our viewing report template, then contact our team using the QR code available in this book. You may want to edit the template, but at least it will provide a framework for you to work from, which should help you in your viewings. It's an 'old school' paper version, but it has helped us over the years build our portfolio. It allows you to make notes on the property whilst on the viewing, but also has a section allowing you to calculate the refurbishment costs. If you're more of an electronic person, then recreate it on a spreadsheet and fill it out on your tablet during your viewings.

It's An Investment

Remember that it's an investment and you are not living there; the investment should purely be based on business principles. For us, the metric we look at is ROCE (Return On Capital Employed). If it's a flip, there needs to be at least £25k in the deal if we are doing a big refurb. If we are planning on using the BRRR strategy, we want to know exactly how much our money will make in 3 scenarios:

- If we receive a low valuation
- If we receive a reasonable valuation
- If we receive a high/ceiling smashed valuation

We also look at cash flow each month. We never invest in a BTL property that is not going to cash flow a minimum of £300pcm; a mini-HMO would need to be a minimum of £600pcm cash flow. Whatever your reasons are for investing, make sure your viewings tick your boxes. If we are doing a flip, then we base the potential profit on the low valuation; anything above is a bonus.

Can I Add Value?

Always ask yourself - can I add any value to this property? Adding value will hopefully allow you to push up the end value and release more of your money. Certain things you can do to add value are:

- Fit a new kitchen
- Fit a new bathroom
- Add/create an extra bedroom
- Open up the kitchen into the dining room and make it an open-plan living space
- Change the layout for more functional living
- Install/upgrade the GCH
- Full rewire with additional sockets, including fresh spotlights in ceilings
- Create parking or additional parking
- Build a dorma
- Create an ensuite (or 2)
- Split the land and sell the plot with planning permission

- For bigger projects, can I get 5 or 6 apartments out of this unit? Can I run an HMO on 1 or 2 floors and create 2 apartments upstairs? The list really does go on.

There are many ways you can add value to property, but you always need to be aware that the amount you spend must generate a sizeable return, i.e., the money you can pull back out of the property or the profit you make.

What Should You Take To Viewings?

Yes, it's a bit geeky, but take a torch on your viewings, a laser measure, and a damp meter. I'm not an expert at diagnosing damp, but we have viewed and invested in enough properties over the years to spot damp. Don't get too scared if the property has damp, like most things in property, money can fix the problem. Just be aware, though, that if the damp is very bad and you are purchasing through a mortgage, they may reduce the amount they lend you. They may 'retain' an amount until the works have been done. In very bad instances, the property may be un-mortgageable, so you will need cash/bridging finance. Don't completely write off these types of properties because there can be great profit in them if you can pick them up at a great price. Taking a step ladder is always best practice so that you can pop your head into the loft space. Needless to say, if you can see daylight or buckets scattered around the loft, you have a roof problem. This may or may not be a big, expensive job, but it still needs to be factored in.

Items we look for during the viewing fall into 2 categories; externally and internally.

Externally

1. **Roof & Chimney:** Are the ridge tiles nice and neat, are there any slats missing, does the roof bow at any part, does the chimney look as if it's been pointed recently? Is it a local meeting place for 100's of pigeons?
2. **Soffits, Facias, Guttering:** Are there any holes in the guttering? Are the facias and soffits old timber? Are there any bits hanging off? Is there a mix and match of old vs new materials? If it's a row of terraces, do you have the downpipe and hopper in front of your house, meaning you're responsible for it (n.b. the best time to look at property is when it's raining).
3. **Garden:** Does it look like a jungle? Are there any large trees where the roots are likely to be underneath the foundations of your property? Are there any signs of Japanese knotweed (Google it)? Are the bushes overgrown and overpowering the garden? Is it a functional garden or is it a 45-degree angle? Don't underestimate the cost of getting a garden back to a clean and tidy state.
4. **The Brickwork:** Does it need repointing (if so, then how many sides), are there any cracks in the brickwork, do any of the lintels above the windows need changing? Are there any cracks zig-zagging their way up the walls? Have any of the bricks failed, i.e., started to crumble?
5. **Windows And Doors:** Are they old timber frames, are they single-glazed, have any of the windows failed (look like they are foggy), are there any cracks?
6. **Porches:** It looks like a complete eyesore and needs to come down. Is it making the house look scruffy?

Internally

1. **<u>Kitchen:</u>** Does it look very old? Is it a functional space, are there enough electrical points, are there old built-in appliances that are on their last legs? Do you need a new one?
2. **<u>Reception room/lounge:</u>** Are there enough electrical points, is the room too big for the single radiator they have in there, and is there adequate lighting? Does the room 'work' for your intended end user.
3. **<u>Electrics:</u>** Is there an old consumer unit with big, old school-style plugs in the bedrooms? Is there only 1 double socket? Are there any single sockets anywhere? Are there any sockets with trunking that are being fed by another socket? Are there sockets in the skirting boards? Are there signs of DIY electrics, upside-down sockets? How is the incoming main feed? Does it look corroded? Does it need replacing?
4. **<u>GCG (Gas Central Heating):</u>** Does it run on GCH or is it old plug-in wall heaters? This then leads to the old water tanks, which often have a back boiler built into the chimney breast. Does it have any GCH? Where is the combi boiler situated – is it in a bedroom or nicely stored in a kitchen, is it in the loft space, how old is the combi boiler, and does it still have the guarantee/warranty? If there is no gas to the property, how far away is it from the street where there is likely to be a main feed?
5. **<u>Bathroom:</u>** Is there condensation/mould build up because the ventilation is not up to scratch, does the suite need ripping out, is the bathroom too big or too small, and could you make 1 of the bedrooms bigger.

6. **Carpet/Flooring:** Is it worn, does it have holes in, does it smell of dogs (I have 3 dogs, so I have nothing wrong with dogs), does it feel like it's as thick as an A4 sheet of paper? Does it feel like the house is leaning slightly to one side? If so, then definitely invest in a structural survey.
7. **Loft:** Can you get into the loft to have a look? Is the loft hatch the size of a pack of cards? Can you see daylight through any of the roof? Are there pigeons in there? Is the insulation up to scratch? Are there holes in the felt? If it's an old terrace, it may not be felted, etc.
8. **Extensions and dorma conversions:** Do they have the building regs sign off and certificate? Does it look like it's more trouble than it's worth?

If it looks like a serious contender, then do a video from the garden/front door and walk through each room of the house. You can talk through the video about things you have noticed in each room, and obviously, what needs improving. When you re-watch the video, you will also notice that you spot other things. Again, this allows you to put in a more informed offer.

The above may seem a bit daunting, but like anything in life, the more you practice, the better you become. Get yourself educated and you will save £££'s on mistakes. Don't shy away from booking viewings, get them booked, and start building up your skill level. The best way to learn is to do. Booking viewings will also get you known amongst the agents, too, and start to build that rapport because it's not what you know, it's who you know. Even better than that is, it's who knows you. You may only be a white belt at viewings, but before you know it, you will be creeping up those coloured belts and soon become a Black Belt. We want you to have a good understanding of the basics of property investing.

Block Viewings

If a property has just gone onto the market and the figures do stack, and you want to book a viewing, but there are loads of people booked to attend, then I would personally leave it. We were interested in a property recently, but when we rang up, there were 21 people already scheduled to attend, and the block viewing wasn't for another 3 days. Of course, the show rate is going to be nowhere near 100% but even if it's 50% that's still about 10 people scrambling over the property. It's fantastic for the agents who are creating that scarcity mindset, but for us as investors, it's no good. Remember that properties come to the market every day, so don't get sucked into the scarcity '*this is the best deal ever' mindset.*' We like smelly, dated properties where we can do a full back-to-brick refurb and add on lots of value. Don't be put off by block viewings because every viewing you go on should be improving your experience and building on the rapport with the agent. If they don't see your face (or your name) regularly, they will forget about you and what you buy.

Get The Inside Information: A Viewing Is Not Just A Viewing

The more viewings you attend, the more agents you speak to, and the more you can ask them questions. Some of the questions we ask are:

- So, have you had much interest in this?
- It's been on for a long time. Why do you think that is?

- Why are the vendors selling? (You may be able to gauge their motivation levels from the answer)
- Have there been any offers accepted?
- I noticed this was off the market, and now it's come back on. Did a sale fall through?
- <after you explain to them the type of property you are looking for> - do you have any properties on your books that fit that description?

A viewing is not just 100% about the property; it should be looked at in light of Pareto's principle, 80/20. 80% of the viewing is in relation to the property, but the other 20% is gathering information from the viewing agent about other properties. When you start to become really experienced, those will flip, meaning 80% is gathering information about other properties. You will often find they say things like

- *'Have you seen this one on X street?' or*
- *'We had a meeting this morning, and we are reducing one tomorrow, you might be interested in', or*
- *'We are taking one on this street, you already have one on there, so would you be interested?'*

It's your job as a professional property investor to try to get the inside knowledge.

In Summary

The only way to get better at viewings is to book them and attend. Just because you are booking a viewing does not mean you are obliged to put in an offer and purchase the property. Learn what to look for and how to make informed decisions.

Chapter 25

How To Know If It's A Good Deal?

A good property deal is not about price alone, it's about aligning the numbers with your personal goals, stress-testing every scenario, and knowing when the risk is truly worth the reward.

You've found a property, is it a deal?

A deal for 1 investor may not be a deal for another, as I have said throughout this book; it's down to the individual investor's goals. 1 investor may want monthly cash flow, another a great ROCE, another a nice lump of cash from a flip, whereas somebody else might just want to park their money somewhere. I have been to several properties where I wouldn't have paid anywhere near what the property has gone on to sell for, but I am sure that if it met the investor's criteria, then they were right to purchase it.

If you are just looking at buying your standard BTLs, then I would be looking at monthly cash flow plus the likelihood of capital appreciation. Now we all know that we cannot accurately predict capital appreciation, but I know if I purchase a property in a bad area, it will not grow as quickly as a property in a great area. Likewise, property in good areas priced correctly sells and rents quickly than those in bad areas.

How Do We Work Out If It's A Deal?

For BRRR, we must lock in profit from day 1. I know so many mentors say *'buy BMV,'* and it's a bit of a cliché, but if you can lock in any profit from day 1 you are really derisking it for yourself. Remember that you should make money when you buy property. Every pound you save on the asking price is a pound of extra equity you have gained.

Step 1: work out how much the property could be worth done up to a good standard, i.e., what's the projected end value

Step 2: calculate how much the refurbishment would cost, plus add on the SDLT, legal fees, and survey fees (breakdown of refurb costs in chapter 39)

Step 3: If there is a large enough difference between those 2 figures, then it's often a deal

Always look to reverse engineer the numbers based on the amount of profit you want from the deal. If you can't make the numbers work, then it's not a deal.

For example:
The property is being marketed for OIRO £160k.

Step 1: A property in that area could be worth £180k when done up to a decent standard
Step 2: the property needs a full new rewire, new kitchen, new bathroom, new central heating system, decorating, and flooring, and you believe you

can get it done for under £20k (good luck with that)
Step 3: There is only £20k difference between the offer/OIRO price and the final price, so it doesn't appear to be a deal

However, It says 'OIRO', so if you secure it at £145k (rather than the £160k), spend £20k on the refurb plus an extra £10k on SDLT, legal fees, and manage to push the ceiling price to £190k, then it could be worth it. The deal would then have a £15-£20k profit, which might work for you and your specific goals.

Some of our best deals have been properties that linger on the market for ages because they need a lot of work, or properties where 1-2 sales have been agreed but then fall through. If you have built a good relationship with your agent through regular viewings and hopefully purchasing from them, and they know you won't let them down, then they can fight your corner to the vendor, saying that they have dealt with you before and you are professional. We have secured a few deals like this because the vendor, having been let down previously, just wanted assurance that the deal would go through.

Only Looking At Cash Flow

Cash flow is a good metric to look at, and we would never be willing to have a property running at a negative monthly cash flow unless we could create some amazing value when the existing tenants move out, i.e., add an extension and change to an HMO, or title split and have two or more units on the same footprint.

You want to ensure good cash flow to allow you to have that pot of money available for maintenance issues when they inevitably arise. When you start to build a portfolio, having an ever-increasing monthly cash flow will also allow you to top up your savings account, which will allow you to reinvest into more cash-flowing assets.

Will It Rent?

You want to ensure that your properties rent ASAP, and they don't linger on the market, forcing you to reduce the monthly rent and thus reduce your monthly cash flow.

You need to check how many properties like yours are available to rent in the area and see how long they have been available. I was speaking to another investor recently, and he was suggesting I look at another area near me, approximately. 30 mins away. I have looked into the area before because properties are about 40-50% cheaper, which is a lot, the rents are about 30% cheaper, so the area is ok to invest in. However, upon close inspection, the number of properties to rent is a lot higher than in our area. There were 42 properties and 12 had 'let agreed', whereas our area has 38 properties, but 22 had 'let agreed'. Like most things, it boils down to the maths. The other area had 12/42 = 28% of properties let, and our normal investment area had 68% let. In the future, we will probably expand into that area if the properties are still considerably cheaper than our normal area, because the ROCE is strong. Black Belt investors listen to more experienced people but also do their own due diligence.

Flipping - Will It Sell And For What Price?

Before you have negative thoughts about the property staying online for years, we must remember that we live on an island where there is a housing shortage, a growing population, and we are selling a product that everybody needs. Your property will sell, but at what price?

The best results we have found are that when the property is a turnkey property, meaning the new owners need to do nothing to it other than turn the key, they sell/rent well. The fact that you are reading this book means that you don't mind the refurbishment side of things because you can see how you can add value, but it takes a rare breed of people who want to actively live on a building site. In my own home, I did it twice; we had a large single-storey wrap-around extension, which involved steel and knock-throughs. Then, 3 years later, we decided to do the same upstairs. Doing it on one of your portfolio properties is a lot easier than a home you live in with your family; it's a lot less stressful.

Just as you had done for your rental demand, you need to do the same for your sale demand. Look for comparables in your area and see the spread, i.e., are 3-bed semi's going for £200-£240k, if so, then what determines that extra £40k? If you are buying to flip, then always calculate backwards based on your ideal profit.

You should find, though, that if you do your refurbishment to a high level, it should obliterate the rest of the competition. Here, though, you still need to be savvy with your numbers, if you had endless amounts of cash, then anybody could keep spending and spending. It's your job to keep your refurbishment budget tight but still create a decent standard.

Stress Test The Deal

You should always do your calculations on the following scenarios. If you are using the BRRR method, then work out

- A low-end value, a medium-end value, and a high-end value.

- Bringing the refurb in on budget, 10% over, 20% over, and 30% over.

If the deal is working with a low-end value and a 130% budget, then the profit should be baked into the deal.

You should do the same for the rental value pcm. How much for an average pcm rent, a good pcm rent, and a ceiling-smashed pcm rent?

Like most things in life, the more experienced you are, the better you will become at analysing deals.

When buying for single lets always work out your rent pcm and compare to the PP, you might be better getting 2 * £100k houses that pay £500 = £1000pcm, vs 1 * £200k that pays £850 = £850pcm = -£150pcm * 12 = £1800pa less per year. However, you must also take into consideration that with 2 properties, you have 2 sets of maintenance, but you also have 2 properties benefitting from capital appreciation.

What Determines If The Deal Is Good?

Below are some factors that determine if the deal is good or not:

- Purchased at the correct price (BMV)
- Bringing the refurb in on budget
- Bringing the refurb in on time
- Adding value far in excess of the cost of the refurb
- High rental demand
- Correct DD done on a like-for-like comparable

In Summary

To decide if it's a deal or not relies on you knowing your own deal metrics and then doing the maths. Just because somebody has told you *'It's a deal,'* it doesn't mean it is; you should carry out your own research and see if it meets your standards and the goals you wish to achieve. Never fudge the numbers to make the deal look better than it is.

Chapter 26

Traditional Financing Strategies

Smart property investors leverage other people's money (OPM) through interest-only mortgages to maximize cash flow, build portfolios faster, and let inflation work in their favour; always aligning mortgage strategy with personal goals and risk tolerance.

Mortgages

A mortgage is a long-term lending product. Mortgages are how most investors best leverage their money. With a mortgage, you are managing to acquire a property by putting down 25% of the agreed sale price (this may or may not be your money, i.e., OPM). In essence, you are borrowing 75% of the agreed sale price and then paying money to the mortgage lender every month.

The most successful property investors leverage OPM, so I suggest you learn how to. Even if you have enough deposit money for 1-10, or even 100 properties, start to leverage OPM so that you can build a bigger portfolio quicker. This took me too long to realise, and as a result, delayed my portfolio's growth.

There are 2 main types of mortgage payment types: interest only and repayment (aka interest and capital)

Interest Only

This is where you are only paying the interest on the money you borrowed, meaning that at the end of the mortgage term, you will still owe the same amount of money you did at the start.

The amount you pay back each month will depend on the interest rate offered and whether it's a fixed or variable mortgage (i.e., the monthly payment can go up and down).

Example for a £100k house based on a 5.5% interest rate

PP	= £100'000
Deposit	= 25% of £100'000 = £25k
Loan	= 75% of £100'000 = £75k
Interest pa at 5.5%	= £75'000 * 0.055% = £4125pa
Interest pcm	= £4'125 / 12 = £343.75pcm

If your anticipated rent was £300 above the £343 (£693), then the property is nicely cash-flowing.

Repayment

This is where you are paying off some of the capital plus the interest. This is known as 'capital repayment'. At the end of the mortgage term, you will not owe anything. Since I had built a very successful Martial Arts School, I was lucky enough to be able to pay off my mortgage at age 29, but because I wasn't that educated, I paid it off at age 33 instead. Stupidly, I liked looking at the money in my account and didn't want it to suddenly drop because I paid off my mortgage. Lack of education, I didn't know what I didn't know. I did not know the power of inflation on good debt. More on paying off your mortgage in the bonus section.

It's good to note, though, that mortgages on capital repayment are top-heavy, which means for the first few years you are paying interest far more than the capital; it's not a 50/50 split. We teach Pareto's 80/20 principle at the Black Belt Academy and how to leverage it best in all areas of your life. The closer you get towards the end of the mortgage, the more the balance tips towards paying off the capital. Lenders do this because they know that you are likely to be with another lender within a few years, so they want to make their money first, i.e, they front-load the payments.

Which Is Best?

This is all dependent on your tolerance for risk, but 99% of property investors have 'interest only' mortgages because they know that inflation will eventually erode their debt. Interest-only mortgages are less pcm than repayment and as such are better for your cash flow. Increasing your cash flow means your funds to reinvest in more property are built up quickly.

During my early days of investing, before I was educated and realised the importance of education, I had 3 properties on repayment mortgages. I did this because it's what my parents advised, what I thought was best, and it's what my accountant advised. I was listening to people who did not have a property portfolio and taking their advice. I urge you to seek advice from people who have achieved what you wish to achieve.

BRRR And Mortgages

If you intend to use the BRRR strategy, then you should purchase the property at first with cash or bridging finance. Once you have purchased the property and done the refurb, you then look to put it on a long-term lending product, i.e., a mortgage. Some of our early deals we wrongly purchased with a mortgage, then did a refurbishment, but struggled to get the correct uplift. Lenders sometimes struggle to see how you can add £30-£70k in value in a few months. If you are ever in that position, you can ask your lender for a further advance, which is when they lend you more money, but you still stay with the same lender.

I've Got £100k Saved Up, Should I Just Buy Outright?

If you are lucky enough to have £ 100'000 sitting in your bank account, then congratulations. Although I am not a financial advisor and am not giving financial advice, I would be putting that money to work ASAP. I would try my best to beat inflation and invest in income-producing assets. I would not just buy 1 single property outright. I have then just depleted all my funds, and only 1 property is increasing in price. I would be looking to split the money up amongst as many deposits as I could. In doing so, I am then growing several properties rather than just 1. Yes, my cash flow might not be as good as with owning 1 property outright, and I have a higher 'good debt' amount, but it's by far the best way to leverage your money. Not pulling out money from a property because you are concerned about a decrease in cash flow is too short-sighted; we need to think long-term, always.

If the property increases in price by 10% a year, then the £100k house you purchased is now worth £110k. However if you had purchased two, then you would benefit from 2 *£10k increase which is £20k, likewise if you had split your money into 3 or 4 properties then you would have increased by £30-£40k. All that additional uplift from the same pot of money. If you have already started to think like that, then well done, you're starting to develop the Black Belt investor mindset.

Good Debt Vs Bad Debt

I was brought up to think that owing money was always bad. I can't complain because it served me very well. I genuinely believe that if people lived well within their means, they would be happier. Buying fancy cars, which I like and which I have had many, that you can't comfortably afford, gets lots of people into trouble. I was not taught about good and bad debt, something that I am teaching my children about continually.

Bad Debt = consumer debt. Debt that is often fixed on things that depreciate. Examples are car finance, catalogue payments, store cards, etc. Things that are '*on the tick*' or '*on the drip*' are often liabilities.

Good Debt = debt fixed against things that often appreciate. Examples are properties.

The good debt and bad debt debate gets many investors questioning paying off their residential mortgage, i.e., '*should I pay it off and reduce my liabilities?*' I can see this from both sides and was lucky enough to be able to pay off my mortgage at a young age. The decision is yours; you need to do what is best for you, your goals, and your life. Paying off your mortgage is a great feeling, knowing you own the property outright is great, but the money is tied up in the property and not working hard for you. Black Belt investors make their money work as hard for them as possible and rarely let it sit idle unless it's part of a bigger plan.

LTV

Loan-to-value. As investors, we currently must put down 25% of the purchase price, so the lender is willing to lend us 75%. Now, if we purchase a property for £100k and have a mortgage of £75k, then we need to fast forward 25 years and think about how much that £75k will actually be worth? This is where you need to understand inflation. I teach my children that when I was growing up, a Mars bar cost 25p and a can of Coke cost 35p/40p. This simple example seemed to help them understand inflation and how things always go up in price. Recently, inflation was roaring away at 8-9% and at 1 point in 2022, it was reported to be about 11% but on average, it is about 2.5% per year. The government has an inflation target of approximately. 2.5% per year because it helps reduce their national debt. That means the £75K will have dropped by 2.5% each year due to inflation. Remember, though, that over the long term, properties increase in price, so your £100k house bought 25 years ago is likely to be worth significantly more. Not only will your house have increased in value, but your mortgage will be relatively small in comparison.

What Do We Do With Our Mortgages?

All our properties are on interest only because we want to build up cash flow to reinvest in other properties. When properties have been in our portfolio 10-15 years, then we may decide to refinance to pull out money to reinvest again, or at least have the option to pay a large amount of the outstanding debt (can't see us doing this, but having the option is nice). What we do may not be best for you, so, like most things in this book, you decide what works best for yourself and your goals.

My Grandads House

In 1973, my grandad purchased his house for £3'600 approx, which I'm sure you will agree was a lot more back then than it is now. Houses on that street are now anywhere from £200k-£250k. If he had had the option to pay the mortgage on interest only, then in 1998, after having the mortgage for 25 years, the £3'600 balance would have been much easier to clear than back in 1973. In 40 years' time, I want to be telling such stories about the 'cheap' properties I bought that are now worth a little fortune. I hope you get to tell those stories to. Remember – it's not '*timing the market*', it's '*time in the market.*'

125% Stress Test

Most lenders stress test that the rent covers your mortgage payment by saying that the rent needs to be 125% of the actual monthly mortgage payment. Therefore, if the mortgage on a single BTL is £500pcm, the rent would need to be 125% of that, which is £625pcm. None of our rentals takes less than £300pcm cash flow, and most are above the £350pcm mark. Be aware, though, that if you are going for larger houses, then don't assume you can pull out a large amount of your money, since the amount they lend you will be based on the rental amount the property will yield. You may have gained an end value of £350k, but the property will only rent for £1000pcm. Therefore, the mortgage will be about £750pcm.

Example for a £350k house based on a 5.5% interest rate

PP (Valuation figure) = £350,000

Deposit (money you need to leave in) = 25% of £350,000 = £87,500

Loan = 75% of £350,000 = £262,500

Interest per annum at 5.5% = £262,500 * 5.5% = £14,443.75 per year

Interest per month = £14,443.75 / 12 = £1,203 per month

As you can see, the rental of £1000pcm does not even cover the mortgage payments of £1203. For the deal to work, the rent would need to be 125% of £1203 = £1503pcm. You are then leaving with £87'500 equity. You need to clearly know your parameters and what you are looking to achieve with each property you purchase. If I had the above property, I would just flip it, have a nice lump of cash, and then reinvest in other properties where I have less money in each deal, but they are producing great levels of cash flow. Link everything back to ROCE.

In summary, most property investors opt for interest-only mortgages because they allow them to increase their monthly cash flow, which allows them to build up deposits to reinvest. They understand the power of inflation and the 'cost of capital.'

Interest Only Or Capital/Repayment?

As I mentioned earlier, this depends on your personal goals. You may want to invest in property to prepare for your retirement so that in 25 years, you have no mortgages. Many people who invest in property already have a great job or a great business, and invest in property as a retirement strategy. They will put the mortgage on a 25-year repayment so that when they retire, the rent from the property tops up their pension. The choice is yours, but it must link to your goals, not somebody else's goals on social media.

I would always use a broker; it's their job to find you the best deal for your situation.

As a property investor, the mortgage lender is going to offer you a 75% LTV. There are some that will offer slightly higher, but not that many that will offer 80% LTV the lender wants you to have 'skin in the game' and reduce their risk.

Fixed, Variable, Or Tracker

If you opt for a fixed rate, then you know what your payments will be each month. Fixed rates are often from 2 to 5 years. However, back in 2021, I knew somebody who locked in a ridiculously low rate for 10 years. It was something like 2.1%! Borrowing money at that rate is outstanding.

Variable rate is the lender's rate, which they often change in line with the Bank of England's base rate. If the BoE rate increases, you can be certain that the following month yours will increase. If it decreases, it may take them a little longer to reduce your payment (it's not in their best interest to pass on the savings to you).

If it's a tracker rate, then it's directly tracked with the BoE rate, so as that fluctuates, so will your payments.

Which is best, you may ask? Again, that is down to you. Personally, we like to fix ours for 3 years. We like to have the reliability of cash flow.

Arrangement Fees

Don't get enticed by the headline rate because the mortgage might have very steep arrangement and valuation fees. You need to look at the overall cost of borrowing rather than just the interest rate. Have a look at this example:

PP = £100k

LTV @ 75% = £75k

Mortgage 1 @ 5% rate with no arrangement fees or valuation fees

Interest pa: £75'000 * 0.05 = £3'750pa

Interest pcm = £312.50pcm

Arrangement fee = £0

Valuation fee = £0

TOTAL PAYABLE = £312.50 * 36 months = £11'250

Mortgage 2 @ 4% rate with 3% arrangement fee and £300 valuation fee

Interest pa: £75'000 * 0.04 = £3000pa (-£750 cheaper)

Interest pcm = £250 (-£62.50pcm cheaper)

Arrangement fee = + 3% of £75'000 = £2'250 (+£2'250)

Valuation fee = + £300 valuation = £300 (+£300)

TOTAL PAYABLE = (£250 * 36 months = £9'000) + £2'250 + £300 = £11'550

As a Black Belt property investor, you should never just look at the interest rate and think *"I'll go with the lowest because it must be the cheapest"*. If I had the option above, I would opt for the 3% arrangement fee because it's only £300 dearer, which over a 3-year period is only £100pa. In choosing that option, I have an increased cash flow of £62.50pcm = £2'250.

Don't be put off by arrangement fees; you need to work out the total cost of borrowing over the length of the term and then make an informed decision.

If you do opt for a repayment mortgage, then your cash flow will be heavily reduced. Yes, with interest only, you're not actually paying anything off the amount, but let inflation erode your mortgage. If you did have the urge to pay off a lump of the capital, then I'm sure the lenders won't turn you down. However, if I had some spare cash lying around, I would be more likely to put it into another passive income-producing asset and grow my wealth.

In Summary

Traditional financing, especially interest-only mortgages, remains the preferred route for most property investors because it maximizes monthly cash flow, enables faster portfolio growth, and lets inflation quietly reduce the real value of long-term debt. While repayment mortgages suit some, especially those using property for retirement planning, it's vital that your mortgage strategy aligns with your personal goals, cash flow needs, and risk tolerance. Understand the full cost of borrowing, not just the interest rate, and always leverage expert advice from brokers, not friends or accountants without portfolios. Smart investors don't just buy property; they buy it with a strategy.

Chapter 27

Why Bridging Finance Isn't As Risky As You Think?

Bridging finance is a strategic tool that accelerates property deals safely when you do your due diligence properly. Don't let perceived risks hold you back from unlocking faster growth and bigger profits.

Bridging finance is just a way of lending money to allow the purchase to go ahead.

Bridging finance, in my experience, has been a much quicker way of purchasing a property compared to a traditional BTL mortgage. The finance is based a lot more on the figures of the deal than it is on you. With a BTL mortgage, it's often a combination of both. There is still paperwork to complete, but often not as much as for a mortgage. Besides, this is your broker's department, so it shouldn't affect you.

Bridging finance is a safe way of borrowing money if you have done your correct due diligence, i.e., done your calculations properly and worked things out on a good, ok, bad scenario.

How Much Does It Cost?

At the time of writing, bridging sits somewhere around 1% pcm. This is dearer than traditional mortgages, but don't step over pounds to pick up pennies. Bridging finance is quicker than obtaining a mortgage, so there is a price to pay for speed. If there is enough profit in the deal, then utilise bridging finance to speed things up.

The BRRR Strategy

If you are implementing the BRRR strategy, then you often purchase the property through bridging finance, or cash (yours or an investor's), and then once the refurbishment has taken place, put the property onto a long-term lending option such as a mortgage.

Don't do what I did back in 2007-2010, which was to purchase a property with a mortgage, carry out the refurbishment, and then try to transfer it to another mortgage. There is the '*6-month rule*' to be aware of. If you did want to do this, then check if your mortgage lender will allow a 'further advance.' This is where your lender will value the property and release more money should they agree that the property is worth more. This, in my experience, has never released as much money as doing it via the bridging route.

Be prepared, though, for the new lender to ask you why you purchased the property 3 months ago for £110k, and now it's worth £170k (that's what happened with one of our properties last year).

When we carry out our refurbishments, we take lots of before, during, and after pictures of every room. This clearly demonstrates that substantial work has been done. Best practice is also to take a video when you start your refurb, during the middle, and then when everything is done. Evidence the refurb as much as possible.

Retained Interest

You must note, though, that the bridging company in 95% of cases will retain your interest payments as soon as they release the money to you. So if you lend £100k and you are expected to pay back £500pcm on a 12-month bridge, then they will retain (keep) 12 * £500pcm = £6k when they release the money. So instead of getting the £100k, you are actually getting £100k-£6k = £94k. I think that's good because rather than having to make payments to the bridging company when the property is being refurbished, your cash flow is better. During the refurbishment stage, the property is a big liability; it's often all pay out, so not having to find the £500pcm interest for the bridge is 1 less thing for you to worry about. Ensure you build in the retained interest into your calculations for the deal.

If you put the property on a mortgage before your bridging period ends, then you will get back any of the retained interest you paid at the start. One of our latest properties, we paid the bridge back by month 7, so we had returned to us the 5 months' interest they kept at the start. We could have paid it back sooner, but we had to abide by the 6-month rule. Always make a note in your diary and/or spreadsheet of when the original bridge amount needs to be paid back, have it as a constant monthly reminder countdown so that you don't get complacent. Delays in property inevitably do happen regardless of your experience, and such delays can cause you penalties, so keep a strict eye on your schedule of works to ensure things are moving as planned.

Bridging Finance Tips

Take out the bridge for 6 months longer than you expect the works and refinance to take. Don't ever take it out based on how long you think the refurb will take, because inevitably delays happen.

Look out for any expensive setup fees, which can make the deal less appealing. For example, they might offer you a 'headline rate,' but once all the additional fees are added, it works out very dear.

When working out your end figures, base it on a worst-case scenario, i.e., you think the property will be worth £200k at the end, do it for 10-15% lower = £170-£180k

Speak to your broker and see what the lender is like if you need to extend the bridge, i.e., penalties. I will not name the lender here in the book, but I know of 1 that other investors have used and said they would never lend from them again. If you are accepted onto the **Black Belt Property Academy,** we share many 'inside secrets' with mentees to help you be more successful.

Start the refinancing process with a new lender towards the end stages of your refurb, do not wait for the refurb to be 100% complete. When we are about 3 weeks away from completing the refurb, we speak to our broker to look at rates, and then we can get one of their valuers out to the site when it's all looking brand new. You must not switch the last 2 R's of BRRR around, don't get a tenant in (rent) before you have got your valuation (refinance). I know what it's like, you just want to get rent coming in to help with cash flow, but you could gain an extra £500 in cash flow, but lose £10k on the valuation. Keep disciplined, ensure you refinance and then rent out.

Regarding bridging rates, just like mortgage interest rates, they do vary. I always look at the end result, though. If we can make a substantial profit and we have to pay a little more in bridging fees, then I won't step over pounds to pick up pennies. Look at the big picture and tie it in with your goal.

In Summary

You need to look at bridging finance as one of the ways you can get hold of the property. If you have done your calculations properly, i.e., the refurbishment costs, made relevant comparables, and worked out worst-case scenarios and the deal stacks, then seriously consider bridging.

Chapter 28

The Creative Finance Toolbox: How To Buy Without The Bank

You don't need a big bank balance to build a big portfolio. You just need the right tools and the mindset to use them. The average investor says, 'I can't afford it.' The Black Belt investor says, 'How can I control it?'"

Let's be clear from the start: creative finance isn't just for people who have no money. It's not a last resort. It's a powerful toolbox used by the wealthiest investors and developers in the world and if you want to build a real property business, you're going to need it.

Most new investors hear "25% deposit" and either try to scrape it together for one deal or give up altogether and go back to the job they hate. But creative finance changes the entire game. It lets you control property without needing your own cash, build faster, and, probably most importantly for you, stop trading time for money.

What Is Creative Finance?

Creative finance isn't one single strategy. It's a way of thinking and a collection of techniques that allow you to acquire and control property using resources beyond your own bank account. It's not magic, it's leverage at its best. Anyone willing to learn and apply it can build a substantial portfolio.

But First; The Mindset Shift

You've probably noticed by now how often I talk about mindset. That's because it *really is* the foundation. And its something we focus on with our mentees. Most investors think:

"I need to save £62.5k to buy a £250k house… I can't do it."

But the creative investor thinks:

"How can I structure the deal so I can control the property now?"

This isn't theory. Study how some of the world's biggest companies operate. Amazon doesn't own most of the products it sells. Airbnb doesn't own the properties. Uber doesn't own the cars. Trump famously took control of entire buildings for $1 before adding value. They focus on control over ownership, and you can do the same in property.

The Creative Finance Toolbox

Creative finance isn't new; it's just that many people haven't heard of it. In the next few chapters, we'll break down six creative finance techniques that can help you build or scale your portfolio:

- Rent to Rent
- Lease Options
- Exchange with Delayed Completion

- Tenant Buyers
- Vendor Finance
- Joint Ventures

Each of these tools can unlock cash flow, give you control, and allow you to acquire assets without needing to put in large sums of capital upfront.

You don't have to use all of them. But the more familiar you become, the more you'll spot opportunities, and the more you'll stack them together to create powerful, win-win deals.

Why Creative Finance Works?

Let's put the numbers in perspective.

As of mid-2025, the average UK house price is £378,000. A 25% deposit is £94,500. Even in more affordable regions where prices hover around £250,000, you're still looking at £60,000+.

Meanwhile, the average savings in the UK are under £7,000.

So it's no wonder that most people never even start their investment journey, or why so many landlords stop after just one or two properties. If you rely purely on savings or traditional deposits, you'll run out of money quickly.

Creative finance is how you grow beyond that point. It's how you stop exchanging years of hard work for every single deal. It's how you build an actual business.

What Makes Sellers Say Yes?

Here's a common question I get asked on the Academy:

"But why would a seller agree to one of these deals?"

Simple. Not everyone is chasing the highest cash offer. Some sellers care more about speed, certainty, income, or reducing stress. Others want the full asking price but don't need all the money now.

That's where your creative structure becomes the solution. If framed correctly, it can give the seller exactly what they need while giving you the deal you want. It's not about being clever. It's about being helpful.

What We Teach Mentees?

Inside the **Black Belt Property Academy**, we tell every mentee the same thing:

"You can waste years trying to figure it all out yourself… or you can study what successful people are doing and copy them."

Creative finance is one of the most important skill sets to develop. I didn't invent these ideas. I've seen firsthand what they can do for your growth. If you're serious about building something long-term, creative finance isn't optional; it's essential.

What's Next?

In the chapters that follow, I'll walk you through each strategy, step-by-step, with examples, structures, and ideas you can actually use.

Whether you're just starting out or looking to break through your next plateau, these techniques will give you more options and more control than any savings account ever could.

But remember: this starts with mindset. You must believe you can. Refuse to let lack of funds, or perceived lack of funds, stop you.

In Summary

Creative finance is not about cutting corners, it's about opening doors. With the right mindset and a flexible toolbox, you can control property, scale faster, and solve real problems for sellers and investors alike. You don't need to wait until you have the perfect deposit, you just need the right approach.

Chapter 29

Rent To Rent

You don't need to own property to profit from it; you just need to control it.

Rent to Rent (R2R) is one of the most accessible ways to start making real money from property without needing huge deposits, credit checks, or a mortgage. You don't own the property, but you control it. You rent it from a landlord at one price and sublet it for a higher amount, keeping the difference as profit.

Usually, you'll do this by turning the property into a multi-let (HMO) or a serviced accommodation unit (SA), increasing the cashflow potential far beyond what a single let would generate.

Done right, R2R can produce thousands per month in income, fast. But let me be clear: this is a cashflow strategy, not an asset-building one. If you stop here, you're not building long-term wealth, you're just building another job. The smart move? Use R2R cash flow to fund your portfolio and grow your real assets.

Although I know quite a lot about R2R, I want to make it clear that I have never used this strategy; I'm not a R2R master, but I am aware of the advantages and disadvantages. We do not teach R2R on the Academy.

Control Without Ownership

The big problem with traditional buy-to-lets is that they're often slow to get moving, and worse, if you're not educated, they don't always cash flow. Between rising interest rates, maintenance costs, voids, and low yields, many landlords are now struggling. That's where R2R comes in.

You step in as a professional operator, take control of a property, improve how it runs, and unlock better returns for everyone involved. You're not breaking the law. You're not scamming anyone. You're offering landlords solutions to problems they may not even realise they have.

Just remember: this is all about control, not ownership. And control is where wealth creation starts.

Don't Say "Rent To Rent"

When you speak to letting agents or landlords, do not say *"Rent to Rent."* It's not that the strategy is bad, it's the perception that can kill the deal before you've even explained anything.

Instead, call it corporate letting or professional property management. R2R has unfortunately been tainted by people attending a weekend course and running out to do dodgy deals. You need to position yourself as a professional. Speak confidently and like someone who knows the business.

How To Find Rent-To-Rent Deals?

You can find deals in two ways: through agents or directly with the landlord.

Through Agents

Treat this like a numbers game. The more calls and viewings you do, the better your chances. Expect 10, 20, even 30 'no' before you get a 'yes'. That's perfectly normal. You don't need everyone to say yes; you only need one to get started.

You must pitch your offer clearly: You'll take care of the property, guarantee rent every month, manage tenants professionally, and remove hassle. That's what many landlords want, especially now.

Direct To Landlord

Platforms like SpareRoom and OpenRent can be goldmines. Look for tired listings, bad photos (bed not made, curtains not open, scruffy, etc), and low engagement. These are your signals that the landlord might be open to a creative solution.

Also, don't ignore the obvious – knock on the door of houses with a "For Sale" sign. If no one's home, knock on the neighbour's door. People talk. You're planting seeds, and persistence wins.

You can also use the HMO register (public information under Section 232 of the Housing Act). Just don't tell the council you're using it to market. When calling landlords from that list, don't say *"I got your number from the register,"* say you found it via SpareRoom or something equivalent.

What To Say (And Not Say)?

As with all interactions and communications, your language matters. Don't pitch on the platform. Ask for a viewing, build rapport, and then discuss your offer in person or privately. I wouldn't register on SpareRoom as a company; they'll bombard you with questions and flag your account. Keep it super lean and friendly.

Remember, many landlords have never even heard of SpareRoom. I read 1 stat somewhere that less than 5% of the UK population uses it. That means the landlords you're competing with for deals aren't even fishing in the right pond.

HMO Licensing & Legal Bits (Without The Boring Stuff)

Yes, you need to understand licensing, but don't overcomplicate it. Whether you're targeting licensed HMOs in Article 4 areas or unlicensed ones outside of it, the opportunity is there. Learn what licensing is required in your area and be 100% compliant. Target landlords who are out of their depth, especially if they're breaking rules without even realising. I spoke to one recently who was selling his small portfolio of HMOs because he was *'sick of all the new laws.'* For old landlords who don't want to bring their properties up to spec, then it's a perfect opportunity for professional investors.

There are new use classes (C5, C6) coming in to clarify shared living, but don't let that scare you. Regulations often create panic, and panic creates opportunity. Just be the calm one who knows how to help.

What This Strategy Really Teaches You?

You don't get wealthy from doing R2R alone, you get wealthy by understanding how and why R2R works, then applying that knowledge to bigger deals.

R2R teaches you how to:

- Build relationships
- Control assets without owning them
- Negotiate win-win deals
- Pitch your value professionally
- Manage cashflow-heavy operations
- Build income that funds real asset growth

If you want a cash-flowing portfolio, this is one of the best places to start because it teaches you how to spot a deal and get control of it, fast.

In Summary

Rent to Rent is one of the most powerful tools in the creative investor's toolbox, but only if you treat it professionally. Use it to generate income, sharpen your negotiation skills, and build relationships with landlords and agents. You mustn't stop there, though; the real goal is to use that cash flow to fund assets you own. Think long-term. Think like a Black Belt investor, not just a hustler.

Chapter 30

Lease Options: Control Now, Buy Later

You don't need deposits, mortgages, or perfect timing, just the right to control the deal.

Most people have done a lease option in some form, they just don't realise it. Think about a car lease: you pay monthly to use the car, and at the end, you can choose whether to buy it, or simply hand it back. Lease Options in property follow the same logic.

It's one of the most powerful creative tools in your property finance toolbox. You gain control now, with the option (not obligation) to buy the property later, often at today's price. That means you can lock in equity, build cashflow, and create upside without needing a mortgage, a big deposit, or bank approval.

Why Lease Options Work?

Let's say you put down a £5,000 option fee and gain control of a property worth £200,000. You agree to buy it in five years, but you're renting it out now, generating monthly income. If the market rises, you've secured a property at a discount. If it doesn't work out, you walk away. That's great leverage, and it's legal.

Control, not ownership, is what smart investors chase.

This is how developers secure land "subject to planning." It's how entire businesses change hands for £1. And it's how many have built serious portfolios without relying on endless 25% deposits.

What's In It For The Seller?

Don't ever lead with "*Would you consider a lease option?*" It'll shut the conversation down fast. Instead, focus on the seller's problem. People don't care about your strategy; they care about what's in it for them.

Build rapport and ask questions. Find out what's really going on:

- Are they relocating but struggling to sell?
- Are they in negative equity?
- Facing repossession?
- A tired landlord with a property sitting empty?

Now imagine saying, "*Between now and the time I buy it, I'll cover your mortgage and bills. You get peace of mind and a guaranteed exit.*" That's not a pitch, that's a solution to their problem, and the right seller will see it as a lifeline.

How To Structure The Deal?

Lease Options aren't a handshake deal. This is a legal, professional agreement and needs to be treated like one. Here's how you typically structure it:

- Agree on a purchase price (fixed now or at a later valuation)
- Pay a small option fee (£1, or a few thousand, depends on the deal)

- Set a term, usually 2 to 5 years
- Agree on monthly payments (sometimes full market rent, sometimes less)
- Decide your exit strategy, will you buy, assign, or walk away?

You can even negotiate to have the monthly rent deducted from the future purchase price. That's right, your rent builds equity in the deal.

How To Find Lease Option Deals?

Lease options aren't advertised. You won't see a sign saying 'Lease Option Available'. You need to read between the lines and do some research.

Look for properties that are both "To Let" and "For Sale", the seller is clearly open to flexibility. Talk to tired landlords, owners of empty homes, and people advertising on free platforms like Facebook Marketplace. In my experience, the more fed up they are, the longer the property has been on the market, the more open they'll be to creative solutions.

The key is rapport. Focus on their situation first and don't talk about the property until you know what they really need.

The Mindset Shift: Control Vs Ownership

The average investor saves £30,000 to put a deposit on a house. What if you used just £5,000 to control a cash-flowing asset today?

You're not buying bricks and mortar, you're buying the rights to a contract that gives you flexibility, leverage, and options. That's how successful investors think.

Legal Protections And Best Practice

This is where most people mess up. Use a proper solicitor who understands lease options; don't ask on social media for a copy of a lease agreement they have used. These protections matter:

- Independent Legal Advice (ILA) for both sides
- Power of Attorney, so the seller doesn't need to show up in 3 years
- RX1 Form, puts a restriction on the title, stopping them from selling or remortgaging behind your back
- Letter of Authority, allows you to communicate with their lender

This is not a grey-area deal. It's a legally binding contract, and it must be treated like one.

Handling Objections Like A Pro

You'll get pushback, which is normal. Here's how to handle it:

"What if you don't pay the mortgage?"

→ "That's the risk you already have now. I'm taking that risk away."

"I want the full asking price."

→ "I might be able to give you more, just not all today. I'll cover your costs now and give you your price later."

"I'd rather wait for a buyer."

→ "That could take 6–12 months, with fees. I can take the headache off your plate now."

This isn't about convincing or trying to con them, it's about presenting a better option, a win-win situation.

Making Lease Options Work For You

Your goal is to create cash flow and optionality. You must make sure your lease option is assignable, so you can sell the contract if needed.

Focus on high-impact, low cost improvements, like turning a 2-bed into a 3-bed. Avoid deep refurbs that tie up too much cash. You want cash flow now, not five years from now.

Market the property properly, manage it like a pro, and never treat it like a short-term hustle.

In Summary

Lease options give you the ability to control property, create cash flow, and secure future wealth without using deposits or mortgages. They're not a trick. They're a legitimate, creative strategy used by some of the smartest investors and biggest businesses in the world. If you want to scale quickly, build flexibility into your portfolio, and get ahead of the game, master Lease Options.

Chapter 31

Exchange With Delayed Completion (EDC)

You don't need more money - you need more time. This strategy gives you both.

Exchange with Delayed Completion (EDC) is one of the most underrated tools in the creative investor's toolbox. It allows you to secure a deal today while completing it later, giving you time to arrange finance, add value, or even find a new buyer. You exchange contracts upfront, so the deal is legally binding, but the final purchase (and full payment) happens down the line. That gap in the middle is where the opportunity lives.

What Is Exchange With Delayed Completion?

Think of EDC as a time machine in your investing journey. It locks in the price and terms now, but delays the completion to a later date — sometimes months, sometimes years. It's commonly called a "long stop completion" by solicitors, but the principle is simple:

- You exchange contracts.
- You delay completion.
- You secure the deal, buy time, and create flexibility.

With normal sales, you don't get the keys until completion unless negotiated otherwise. With EDCs, though, you must get keys on exchange, so this is something you must negotiate with the current vendors.

Why Use EDC?

Not every seller needs all their money today. In fact, most fall into one of three categories:

1. They need all their money now
2. They need some of it now
3. They need none of it now

EDC works perfectly for groups 2 and 3. You're solving their problem while giving yourself time to solve yours.

Structuring The Offer

When speaking to a seller, always give them two offers:

1. Cash offer now (X)
2. Higher offer over time (Y)

This avoids a simple yes/no outcome. If they say, *'Why not just buy it now?"* - your answer is easy: *"We can, but that would be for the lower amount."*

An EDC can also be a natural fallback when someone isn't quite ready for a lease option. If they're unsure about creative deals, suggesting an EDC with proper legal structure can feel safer for them, and still give you time flexibility.

Legal Points To Remember

Let me say it here again: always seek professional advice. I am not a solicitor, tax advisor, or accountant and Im only sharing my experience.

- SDLT is payable on substantial completion. If you get the keys at the exchange, you'll likely trigger SDLT, not because the law changed, but because solicitors prefer to wrap everything up early for admin ease.
- Always use specialist solicitors who understand EDCs. If they advise against it, and you are still confident you want to go ahead, you can say: "*Thanks for the advice, please proceed.*" Their job is to protect their liability, not help you achieve your goals.
- EDCs offer more protection than lease options because solicitors have to be involved. That structure ensures IDA, contracts, and accountability are all in place.

Instalment Contracts & Creative Terms

An EDC doesn't mean you do nothing in the meantime. You might:

- Pay monthly instalments to cover the mortgage and reduce the future sale price
- Add tenant buyers or make minor improvements
- Stack EDC with other strategies (vendor finance, lease options, etc.)

Example: You agree to buy a house in 5 years. In the meantime, you pay £350/month, where £300 covers mortgage interest and £50 reduces the purchase price. That £50/month chips away at your future balance — meaning you're buying time *and* equity.

Mindset Shift: Think Like A Problem Solver

Stop assuming sellers think like you; a very high percentage of sellers don't read books on property investing. Some are overwhelmed, some are desperate, some just want peace of mind. Your job is to be part investor, part social worker. Sit with them & listen to them. Help them see their situation clearly, even write it down for them. In many cases, you're not just making an offer, you're offering relief, clarity, and a way out. Everything you do, though, must be ethical and a win-win.

Key Reminders When Using EDCs

- Don't tell solicitors absolutely everything about the deal. Give them clear instructions, not your full backstory or creative knowledge. They just need to know the essentials of the deal
- People invest in you, not just the deal, so show up professionally
- This is about return on time and creativity, not just capital. Focus on ROCE, and you might meet triple-digit returns with minimal input
- Don't try to work it all out on the first visit. Just get to the next step

Common Use Cases

- You need time to sell another property or raise finance
- The vendor wants to sell but isn't in a rush for full payment
- Planning gain, flips, or tenant buyer strategies are in motion
- You want to tie up a deal in a hot area before the price rises

Remember, if you're dealing with short-lease flats, you often need to own it for two years before extending. So a delayed completion might just give you the leverage you need without rushing to buy.

Building Your Edge

EDCs work especially well when you know your area inside out. That local knowledge about the good streets, the bad ones, the motivated sellers, gives you an edge money can't buy. It's not about your bank account. It's about how creatively you can structure a deal. You don't need to buy a mortgage; you can make money by taking over one.

In Summary

Exchange with Delayed Completion lets you secure today's deals using tomorrow's money. It buys you time, flexibility, and a massive strategic edge, all while offering a win-win to the seller. Whether you're building your pipeline, juggling finance, or stacking other creative tools, EDC is a legal, powerful strategy used by some of the savviest investors in the game. It's not about owning everything now, it's about controlling it smartly, and completing when the time is right.

Chapter 32

Tenant Buyers: Get Paid To Sell Later

You don't need to own the house forever; you just need to own the right to profit from it.

One of the most underrated ways to generate upfront income, passive cash flow, and a future exit is by using tenant buyers. This strategy flips the traditional landlord model on its head: instead of taking on long-term tenants and dealing with maintenance, you install someone who wants to own the house… just not today.

They live in the property, treat it like their own, and pay:

- A normal monthly rent
- A monthly top-up (which could go toward their future purchase)
- An upfront option fee (non-refundable)

It's the perfect hybrid of short-term income and long-term planning. You're not just a landlord here, you're a seller in waiting.

What Is A Tenant Buyer?

A tenant buyer is exactly what it sounds like: someone who starts as a tenant and becomes a buyer later down the line. It's often used alongside a lease option agreement, giving them the right (but not the obligation) to buy at a fixed price in the future.

For you as the investor, it means:

- No maintenance calls at 10 pm or on weekends
- No management fees
- No voids caused by casual renters
- And you get paid upfront for giving someone a shot at ownership

They behave like homeowners because they plan to be homeowners.

Why Use Tenant Buyers?

Let's be honest, some properties don't cash flow well as single lets. If you BRRR a property and leave £10k–£15k in the deal, you're tying up cash that could be used elsewhere. With a tenant buyer in place, you gain:

- Higher monthly income (thanks to the top-up)
- A large option fee upfront (often thousands)
- Zero maintenance liability
- A clear exit that you've already agreed to upfront

If, for some reason, they don't complete later on, you've had all the benefits along the way, and you still own the asset. This is how you boost your cash flow, especially when paired with creative strategies like Lease Options or Exchange with Delayed Completion.

Creative Deal Structuring With Tenant Buyers

This isn't about "cheap houses only," you can use this strategy at the top end of the market too. I've heard of one investor who controlled a £2 million mansion with just a creative approach. They agreed a sale of less than the £2 million, they provided a loan from their business to the sellers business, in the process legally saved thousands in tax.

These aren't tricks; they're smart, legal structures designed to solve both parties' problems. The truth is, you don't need to buy expensive properties; you need to structure them. That's the power of creative finance.

How This Builds Wealth, Fast?

Let's say you're clearing £1,000 a month on a tenant buyer deal. Over two years, that's £24,000, which is nearly enough for a 25% deposit on a traditional £100'000 BTL, if you even want to go that route. Instead of grinding to save money for a house deposit the old-fashioned way, you're building deposits from cash flow. Let the deal fund the next deal; this is how creative finance scales.

Mindset And Marketing Go Hand In Hand

You can't rely on strategy alone; you need people to know you exist. You don't need to go on an all-out marketing mission, but let people know what you do and how you can help.

If you haven't already:

- Get your CRM system linked to your website (get a basic website)
- Start building email nurture campaigns
- Implement follow-ups automatically

As Gary Vee says, attention is currency. If no one knows who you are, you'll have to work twice as hard for every lead.

Don't Forget…

You're not doing this to play landlord. You're building assets that pay you for life. You're building freedom, options, and a portfolio that can fund your future. One of the best bits is you're helping people along the way, giving them a real shot at homeownership, without needing a deposit today. That's a win for them and a win for you.

In Summary

Tenant Buyers give you cash today, cash flow tomorrow, and an agreed sale in the future, all while removing the headaches of traditional renting. The upfront option fee helps recover your capital quickly. The monthly top-up boosts your returns, and with no maintenance or management costs, you keep more of what you earn.

This isn't just about making more money; it's about doing less work for better results. Combine Tenant Buyers with other creative tools like Lease Options or EDC, and you've got a fast-track to wealth that's built on control, not cash.

Chapter 33

Vendor Finance: When The Seller Becomes The Bank

Why use the bank for money when the seller might lend it to you themselves?

Most investors never even consider asking the seller to help fund the deal, which is exactly why most investors stay stuck. Vendor Finance (also known as Seller Finance) is a powerful tool in creative property investing. Rather than taking out a mortgage and handing over a large deposit, you negotiate directly with the seller, allowing them to become your lender.

The concept is very simple, but the impact is enormous. You agree a price, but instead of borrowing from a bank, the seller agrees to be paid in instalments. You control the property, cash flow from day one, and only need to pay the balance off at an agreed future date, often without interest.

This is not a theory. This is being used right now by smart investors to acquire properties with no traditional lending, minimal capital, and total control.

Why Would A Seller Agree To This?

It's easy to assume every seller wants all their money up front. In reality, some don't. Some are downsizing, retiring, or simply looking for ongoing income rather than a lump sum. Others want to avoid a heavy capital gains tax hit by spreading the sale over a number of years. There are even sellers with unmortgageable properties, ones most buyers walk away from, who just want to be done with it.

Vendor Finance becomes a win-win when:

- The seller owns the property outright or has little mortgage left
- They value peace of mind and income over urgency
- You're offering a solution, not just an offer

Your job is to uncover their priorities. What are they really trying to achieve; cash, convenience, or certainty? When you lead with those questions, you find creative answers that work for both sides.

What Does It Look Like In Practice?

Let's say you agree to buy a property for £200'000. You offer:

- £5'000 upfront as a commitment fee
- The remaining £195'000 paid over five years
- Monthly payments of £1'000, with a balloon payment at the end

You now control the asset, rent it out at £1'500 per month, and pocket £500 as monthly cash flow or put it to 1 side to pay off the balance. The seller receives steady income, no hassle, and the security of knowing their money is coming.

At the end of the five years, you refinance, sell, or use another strategy to pay off the outstanding balance. The seller gets their full price. You've built equity, income, and control, without ever asking a bank for permission.

The Key Ingredient: Trust, Framed Professionally

While this is a relationship-driven strategy, like all the other creative strategies, it's not based on handshakes. Just like a mortgage lender, most sellers will want:

- A formal contract
- A legal charge on the property
- A clearly defined repayment schedule

This should all be handled via solicitors. Just because it's creative doesn't mean it's casual. Vendor Finance is a real transaction, with legal protections and clear outcomes. Treat it with the professionalism it deserves.

Why This Strategy Is So Powerful?

Vendor Finance gives you control of an asset with minimal capital input. You can:

- Acquire unmortgageable or unusual properties
- Avoid the need for large deposits or immediate refinancing
- Negotiate flexible terms to suit your business plan
- Create income from day one

It's especially powerful when combined with other strategies, Lease Options, Tenant Buyers, or Delayed Completion. This approach unlocks deals others walk away from, not because you have more money, but because you understand more ways to structure a win.

When you can confidently sit down with a seller and offer multiple ways to help them, you stop being just another buyer, you become a problem solver.

In Summary

Vendor Finance turns the seller into the lender, giving you control of the deal with minimal upfront cost. This isn't a loophole; it's a respected, legal strategy used by seasoned investors to scale faster, reduce reliance on banks, and structure deals others don't even see.

The seller wins with income and a fair price. You win with cash flow, control, and time to execute your exit. By understanding what the seller truly needs and presenting creative solutions, you move from competing on price to leading with value.

Creative Finance is not about money. It's about Black Belt mastery.

Chapter 34

Joint Ventures: How To Fund Deals Without A Mortgage

You don't need all the money. You just need to know how to bring value.

Most people are stuck waiting for their capital to catch up with their ambition. They've got deals they can't fund, momentum they can't maintain, or growth that's frustratingly slow. The truth is, you don't need to fund every deal yourself. What you need is to understand the power of Joint Ventures, where two or more parties come together to achieve more than they could alone.

This isn't about borrowing, it's about partnering. One person brings the funds, the other brings the opportunity, expertise, and execution. When done properly, JVs are one of the fastest ways to scale your portfolio, build wealth, and gain experience while delivering value to others.

What Does A Joint Venture Look Like In Practice?

Joint Ventures come in many forms, but the principle is always the same: both parties bring something to the table and agree on how the rewards will be shared.

You might be the one finding the deal, managing the refurb, handling the tenants, and overseeing the legal process. Your JV partner might provide the deposit, the refurb funds, and any associated costs. Together, you agree on the structure, a flip with shared profits, a long-term hold with cash flow split, or a refinance and equity release.

The key is that the arrangement works for both sides. Some investors want hands-off returns. Others are happy to contribute knowledge and effort in exchange for future upside. The beauty of a JV is that it can be tailored to fit the people involved, not forced into a rigid one-size-fits-all box.

The Most Common JV Structures

While every partnership is unique, most JVs fall into one of three categories:

- Money Partner JV – One person funds the entire deal; the other runs it day-to-day. Profits are shared as agreed.
- Equity JV – Both parties contribute a mix of cash, time, or skills. Returns are split based on the value brought in.
- Sweat Equity JV – One party owns the asset; the other adds value through refurbishment or management and earns a share of the uplift or income.

It's not about who brings more, it's about making sure both parties are aligned, protected, and clear on the outcome.

What Makes A Joint Venture Work?

The most successful JV relationships are built on clarity and trust. Before any money changes hands, both parties should agree in writing on the exact structure of the deal. This means:

- Having a solicitor-drafted agreement
- Agreeing on the objective, is this a flip or a hold?
- Outlining a clear exit plan, what happens if one party wants to exit early?

Many JV horror stories come from vague arrangements, verbal agreements, or mismatched expectations. These are real businesses and as such they require structure, communication, and legal protection.

That being said, people don't invest in documents; they invest in people (it's that old 'know-like-trust' cycle). If you want to raise capital through Joint Ventures, your focus should be on becoming investable. Show people why you're the right person to trust with their money, show them you're educated. That means showing past deals, highlighting results, being honest about your process, and showing that you can be relied on from start to finish.

This Is The Fuel That Scales Your Portfolio

Running out of capital shouldn't be the reason you slow down. If your deal flow is strong, if you've proven your ability to find and deliver returns, then Joint Ventures become the natural next step.

JVs allow you to:

- Leverage your experience and systems to create more income
- Help others grow their wealth without them doing the heavy lifting
- Build long-term relationships with repeat investors

Don't wait for someone to offer you money because if you do, it might not ever happen. You must be proactive. Start sharing your journey, talk about what you're working on, and be open about the type of partners you're looking for. People with money and who understand it are constantly looking for better returns. What they need is confidence, credibility, and a clear offer.

In Summary

Joint Ventures are not about needing money. They're about building something bigger, together. One person brings the funds, the other brings the deal and the drive. When both are aligned, you get speed, scale, and synergy, the three ingredients most investors are missing.

Success comes from being clear, credible, and committed. If you want someone to fund your deals, prove you know what you're doing, protect their money like your own, and always act like a professional. This is how you go from doing one deal at a time to creating consistent, compounding growth with partners who back you again and again.

Chapter 35

Stacking Strategies: Combining Creative Finance For Bigger Wins

When you stop playing with one tool at a time and start stacking strategies together, that's when deals get exciting, scalable, and extremely profitable.

Most investors learn one creative strategy and then stay in that lane. They might master Rent-to-Rent, Lease Options, or Joint Ventures, but never think to combine them. That's like owning a full toolbox and only ever using the hammer. Of course, we need to be competent at 1 strategy, but we should expand our repertoire of skills to help grow the portfolio you want.

The truth is, the best deals often come from layering two or more creative strategies together. This is called "*stacking,*" and once you understand how to mix and match the right tools, the potential is enormous. You create more value, solve more problems, and structure deals that other investors simply wouldn't see. If your only tool is that you need a 25% deposit, then you're limiting your growth.

What Is Strategy Stacking?

Strategy stacking is the art of using multiple creative finance tools in the same deal to reduce your capital input, increase your upside, and solve more seller or buyer problems in one go.

It might look like this:

- Taking on a property with a Lease Option, then finding a Tenant Buyer to live in it and pay you a fee
- Securing a deal using Exchange with Delayed Completion, and funding the refurb through a Joint Venture
- Acquiring a property through Vendor Finance, then selling it via an Assisted Sale to a tenant buyer or homeowner
- Combining Rent-to-Rent with Company lets to maximise commercial cash flow

Each one of those strategies works in isolation. But when you combine them intelligently, the deal becomes stronger, more profitable, and often faster to execute. It's about getting more from less, squeezing every bit of value from the opportunity. You need to make sure every £1 is working hard for you.

Why Strategy Stacking Works So Well?

When you combine strategies, you're not just looking for a discount or trying to save your own money. You're identifying pressure points on both sides of the transaction and matching them with the right tools.

Let's say a vendor wants a fixed price, but doesn't need the money now. You could offer a Lease Option with an agreed price and monthly payments. Then you put in a Tenant Buyer, who pays you a fee and a monthly top-up covering the cost, and gives you instant cash flow.

You've:

- Gained control of the property
- Generated upfront and ongoing income
- Helped a seller move on
- Given a buyer a route to ownership
- Built a long-term asset position for yourself

All without using traditional mortgages, big deposits, or even ownership, at least not at the start. This is the power of stacking, and when done properly, can transform simple deals into long-term wealth generators.

Stacking In The Real World: A Quick Example

Let's break down a stacked deal to show how this works in real life:

- A tired landlord is struggling to let a house and doesn't want to deal with agents anymore.
- You agree a Lease Option of £1'000 option fee, £750pcm for 3 years, purchase price locked at £175'000.
- You advertise and find a Tenant Buyer who pays a £5'000 option fee and £950pcm (of which £200 is a monthly top-up).
- You invest the £4'000 upfront, and an extra £200/month in cash flow.

- At the end of the term, the buyer gets a mortgage, pays you £175'000 (or more), and you exercise your option with the original seller.

In this deal, you never used a mortgage; you didn't need a big deposit. You solved two people's problems and got paid multiple times for doing so, upfront, monthly, and at exit. I hope you're starting to get excited about the opportunities that are available to you.

Start Thinking In Combinations

If you want to get ahead in property, you need to start seeing property as a puzzle and creative finance as your set of tools to solve it. Every seller has different motivations, and every property has its own challenges. When you understand how the different strategies work together, you become a problem-solver, not just a buyer. The more combinations you understand, the more flexible you become. The key is not to force it. Listen first, understand what the seller or vendor truly needs, then pick and stack the strategies that solve the problem while protecting your downside and growing your upside.

In Summary

Stacking strategies is how creative investors go from surviving to scaling. Each tool we have briefly covered, Lease Options, Tenant Buyers, Vendor Finance, Delayed Completion, JVs, has power on its own. But when combined, they create exponential results. You reduce risk, unlock bigger deals, and often generate three or four income streams from one asset. Most investors never get this far. They stop at one strategy and never explore the next level. If you want to build wealth faster, control more property with less capital, and stay ahead of the competition, then learn to stack, adapt, and always look for the win-win. That's how portfolios are built.

PART 5

From Purchase To Profit: The Refurb Process

This is where your plans turn into profit. In this section, we walk through the full process from the moment you agree to buy a property to the point it's refurbished, revalued, and ready to deliver returns. You'll learn how to navigate conveyancing, understand the true costs of buying, plan effective refurbishments & manage tradespeople. It's about doing the right work, in the right way, to maximise value and move confidently toward your financial goals.

Chapter 36

How Investors Avoid Conveyancing Disasters?

Getting your offer accepted is only the beginning; the real battle is avoiding problems during the conveyancing process. You must stay sharp, stay proactive, and let the professionals do their job while you focus on the next deal.

Getting an offer accepted should feel great; you are a step closer to increasing your wealth and your monthly cash flow. If you have followed my advice, you have locked in profit from day 1. Unfortunately, having your offer accepted is step 1 of the conveyancing process, and currently in the UK 1 out of 3 properties that have an offer accepted '*fall out of bed*'. You may be gazumped or have to pull out of the sale yourself. It's my advice that you should still attend viewings and still be actively looking at properties that fit your investment criteria, just in case yours falls through.

Your role during the conveyancing process is to answer any questions the solicitors have asap and not to panic. Of course, have regular check-ins with the progress, but other than answering their questions and providing what is needed, you can't do anything else other than wait.

Stages Of A Sale

Choose A Solicitor

If you have not used a solicitor previously for a property purchase, then speak to other investors in your area and see who they would and wouldn't use. At the time of writing, we have just completed a property, and the sellers' solicitors were very slow. According to our solicitors, they are notoriously slow. I obviously learned from this that we will not be using them for future purchases should anything deteriorate with our current solicitors. Remember that somebody telling you that there is a solicitor at the bottom of their street does not mean they are a good one; they are just telling you general information. At the minimum, check out Google reviews and speak to estate agents and ask who they think is quick at getting things done. I would not go for an online-only solicitor because I want to be able to speak to the same case handler throughout the process. Our solicitor is in our local town, and I can drop things off and sign things without having to delay the process. If you are dealing with a solicitor who is too far away, this becomes an obstacle. Like most things in business, it will be trial and error. A solicitor is a good part of your power team, so once you find one that returns your calls and emails, keep them close.

Let Them Know About The Sale

If you already have a solicitor, then contact them and your broker to agree on the purchase price and the address. Provide them with as much relevant information as you can to prepare them.

Memo Of Sale

A memorandum of sale created by your estate agent is often sent to your solicitor, but I would always send one anyway. The memorandum of sale simply identifies the property address, the buyer's and seller's name, their solicitors, and the purchase price.

ID Checks

Early on in the conveyancing process, the solicitors often want you to do an ID check; they may ask you to download an app like Thirdfort. Over the years, these have become more and more efficient. The last one we did took about 5 minutes. You often need to take a picture of your passport or driving licence via your smartphone, then put your smartphone next to the biometric bit of your passport.

Maybe Funds

The solicitor may ask for some funds to take things a step further. Funds are likely to be for searches; they may refer to these as 'disbursements.'

Draft Contracts

The seller's solicitors then prepare draft contracts. This contract pack will include the draft contract and any other documents your solicitors are likely to need.

Searches

Searches are frequently done at this stage and normally consist of local authority searches, other environmental searches, and water and drainage checks. Searches are often a mandatory requirement from lenders to see if there are any issues with the property you need to be aware of. If there are any problems with the searches, the lender may not lend or put a restriction in place.

Surveys

Around this time, you may have a survey, and the results of which may mean you adjust the purchase price offer or decide to pull out of the property sale. Having a survey done can be a good bargaining tool because if the surveyor says there is a problem with damp and it will need £3k to rectify, you should then go back to the agent and say "*I need to revise my offer based on this new information*". A majority of the time, the seller realises that other people who have a survey done will also find the same information and may ask for the same reduction, and they often agree to the reduction.

Initial Enquiries

Initial enquiries are normally raised by your solicitor based on the draft contract, the search results, and other items the seller's solicitor may have included. Be aware that if they are waiting for replies to initial enquiries, you should get in touch with the estate agent, who can also chase the vendor to chase their solicitors. Try to be proactive instead of reactive.

Mortgage Deeds And Mortgage Offer

You will need to sign the mortgage deeds and the mortgage offer, and this can be done with the solicitors or without them. The last few purchases we have made, we have signed and scanned the paperwork back from our office. Most times, they ask you not to date the deeds.

Exchanging Contracts

If all is going well, you should now be close to exchanging contracts. If the seller's solicitor answers any questions your solicitor asks and your solicitor is still happy, then contracts can be signed, and money can be transferred. Both solicitors sign and exchange contracts, and that's it.

Completion

The final stage is completion, which is when all monies are transferred. The completion date is when ownership is transferred to the buyer. Make sure you save all the documents your solicitor has provided you with, especially the TR1 form, which is proof of ownership. You will need the TR1 form when you come to refinance.

Best Practice During The Conveyancing Stage

- Be ready for and expect delays and obstacles. Your job as a Black Belt property investor is to overcome these obstacles so that you acquire great assets at fair prices (not fair assets and great prices).
- Always email the solicitors weekly so they know you are still there and still keen. We block out reminders to email the solicitors on the same day each week until the sale goes through. This isn't being annoying; it's letting them politely know you want to get things moving and that you are professional.
- Email the estate agents the day after contacting the solicitors to provide them with an update. You want to come across as professional to the agents, especially if it's the first time you are purchasing through them.

A team saying I used to have in my Martial Arts School, *'give an update even if there is no update'* – the same applies when buying houses.

- Continue to build relationships with the agent by going on more viewings. Ensure the viewings are properties you are genuinely interested in. You should do this to let the agent know you are keen, plus if anything happens with the current sale going through, you should have a good deal flow.
- Each solicitor might blame the other solicitor for being slow and holding the process up. If you are touching base with them every 7 days, this should be less of an issue, but be aware that it can happen
- If you are purchasing through a bridging loan, then try to make sure the money lands as close to the time your solicitors are likely to need the money. We have done this previously and have asked the solicitors dealing with the bridge to complete 7 days before we were due to complete on the investment purchase. You don't want to have all that money in your account because as soon as it lands, you start paying interest on it. Paying 1 week's interest is much better than paying 1-2 months' interest.
- You need to visit the solicitors if they are local to sign the mortgage deed & mortgage confirmation
- If you are purchasing in a company name, you will need to get ILA (Independent Legal Advice described earlier in the book), and all directors will need to complete one

Be aware that the house might not be empty, so you need to line up removal/house clearance contractors. Never assume it will be empty upon key collection, so always clarify if it's going to be fully emptied or 'sold as seen'.

You might need to visit the solicitor more times to sign things, even though the solicitor said that they have everything and you don't need to come in again.

Be aware that the property is not being registered – you will need to do that upon completion.

ILA

If you are buying in a LTD company, you will need to seek Independent Legal Advice (ILA). This means you need to go to another solicitor firm, which will have to go through the documents that the mortgage company has asked you to sign. You will be required to sign a PG (Personal Guarantee), and this should not be something you worry about if you 100% intend to pay the mortgage each month, which, of course, I'm sure you do. Signing a PG means that if your company goes belly up, you are still obliged to pay the mortgage.

When Is SDLT Paid?

Currently, you can pay this up to 14 days after completion, but every solicitor we have used has this built into the completion statement, so it's all paid in 1 transaction. Again, don't worry, this is down to your solicitors to sort out, that's what you are paying them for.

Once our solicitor had sent a completion statement without the SDLT, it was a nice surprise, but at the same time, I knew it wouldn't just disappear. As much as we'd like to save the SDLT, you are best off just notifying your solicitor, who will then amend accordingly.

When Do You Pick Up Keys?

Remember that the estate agent needs to confirm that the vendor has received the funds and that keys can be released (you may have transferred the money, but that doesn't mean you can go straight to the estate agent). Don't think that once you have transferred your money and you have completed that, you can go to collect the keys. Always contact the selling agent to confirm that the seller has received the funds, and you can collect the keys.

No EPC

Most agents will have noticed it doesn't have an EPC before listing it, but sometimes it is forgotten about. If it doesn't have an EPC, then contact the agent to get one organised, which will be at their/the seller's expense. If the EPC is an E or F, then you will be restricted in lenders for your BTL mortgage. If the EPC is ridiculously low, like a 'G', then offer lower because of the additional fees you will incur from having to take out bridging finance. However, you should have calculated this in your offer.

<u>In Summary</u>

Understanding the process is great, but you need to leave the conveyancing process to the professionals. You may want to speed things up, but all you can do is trust the process and reply to any of their questions asap.

Chapter 37

Fees: The True Cost Of Buying Property

Fees are the price of entry to the property game, know them, plan for them, and treat them like any smart business owner would: as necessary steps on your path to long-term wealth.

In the world of property investing, there are lots of fees that you will encounter. Most of the time, these fees are unavoidable. If you think you will just buy a £100k house with a small deposit, then rent it out and watch the money come in each and every month, then I have some bad news: it's a bit trickier than that. Of course, there are lots of creative NMD ways you can control a property, some of which I've briefly covered in this book, but whatever the acquisition method, there will be varying levels of fees to pay. Even if you are doing a purchase lease option (PLO), there must still be a monetary exchange. Yes, this might be as little as £1, but you still want a specialist solicitor to draft up and approve your lease option.

Please don't be put off, though. Mindset is crucial, so you need to understand that many people who don't invest in property will be telling you not to waste your money. If you are educated and have done your due diligence, then you will have factored all of the fees into the deal and worked out if it has enough profit margin for you to progress. I'm an active property investor, and although there are fees to pay, if you know what you are doing, you should build on your wealth and passive income every year.

As with any business, there are expenses that you will incur; you decide how granular you want to go with tracking these expenses, but even before the viewing stage, you have expenses such as travel time, time on the phone booking the appointment, research time, printing expenses, fuel expenses, etc. We don't track any of these other than fuel, but over time, regardless of how small and insignificant they may be, they will add up. If you employ a virtual assistant to help you run your business, then that must be tracked and recorded. We do record every expense that we incur, though, because we should never make our business look better than it actually is. For example, if you meet a broker once a month for a coffee and an investor once a month, those 2 coffee receipts should go on your expenses and come off your profit for that year. I'm a systems man, so in the Black Belt Property Academy, we heavily encourage mentees to record every single expense they incur. Tracking expenses is not 'tight,' it's having good business sense.

After your viewing and your offer being accepted, you then have the conveyancing fees to start with. When you have agreed on a sale, here are some of the fees you are likely to have to pay

Broker Fee – £FREE-£400

I've worked with a few brokers over the years, but the one we are currently working with does not take a fee until we complete. This is brilliant for us because we don't have to pay anything until the deal is over the line. Some brokers want a fee to start, but I wouldn't really say one way is better than the other. I'm just wary of paying fee after fee and not really getting anywhere. I wouldn't begrudge your broker their fee because they have access to funding, and they complete a lot of paperwork and answer lenders' questions behind the scenes without you having to get involved. This links back to your power team, but when you find a great broker, build on the relationship because they can help you grow.

Legal/Solicitor Fees – This Is Approx £1200-£2k

You will be able to get them much cheaper, maybe through some sort of online solicitors, where all communication is via email. I'm a firm believer that you get what you pay for, so if they are really cheap, there will be a reason for this. The solicitor we use has done several purchases for us, and we know most of their small team. I can drive to their office and speak to an actual person (not an online live chat) and often get answers there and then. What I don't want is to be part of some '*sausage factory*' where I never speak to the same person twice, and I'm constantly having to repeat the same information on every phone call over and over again. I'm a great believer of '*don't step over pounds to pick up pennies*' – I'd rather pay that bit more to know the job will get done properly and in an efficient manner.

Application Fee – £FREE-£300

Certain lenders require an application fee to be paid upon applying for a mortgage or bridging finance. You have to pay for them to look at your application. If the rate/deal is that good, then I would pay the fee because the profit is in the deal. If the deal is too tight, then I wouldn't be going for it, and second, I would not want to be paying application fees.

Survey – £250-£1500

There are different levels of surveys you can have done, each going into varying depths. We never do L1 surveys because I personally feel they are a little pointless; these are about £250 approx. A level 2 survey is a home buyer's report and is £350 approx. A level 3 survey, known as a full building survey, which is the one we tend to have because we tend to buy fairly run-down properties, is approximately £1000. If you have a bad feeling about the house and still want to go ahead, then I would go all out and get the most extensive survey done possible. If anything comes back, which it most likely will because the surveyor will have gone into great depth and wouldn't want you thinking you have paid lots of money for a pointless document, then use this as a bargaining tool to negotiate more money off the purchase price. If you explain that any future buyers will probably find the same thing, then they often just agree to reduce it by the amount the surveyor has suggested the works will cost. If you do see lots of red on the survey, then don't panic; it doesn't necessarily mean the house is falling down; it just means there are issues that need to be addressed. The more red items on the report, the more you should be able to reduce the purchase price.

Searches – £250-£500

These can often appear as trivial procedures and a box-ticking exercise, but regardless, they need to be done during the conveyancing process. Searches carried out are local authority, coal mining, environmental, draining, etc. Lenders require these, so you just have to bite the bullet. The fees, though, are often paid in advance just in case the sale falls through. However, I have had to pay a separate agency from my solicitor previously because the solicitor wanted to stay out of the payment side of things.

Outstanding Ground Rent – £0-£200

If you are buying a leasehold property, there may be some outstanding ground rent to pay. We tend to buy properties that are 80-120 years old, so the ground rent is often marginal, i.e., £3 per year. Depending on the amount of debt, you need to decide if it's just worth you settling the amount or trying to chase up the person whose debt it is. If it's ground rent of about £9, then fine, we will cover it. If it's something up to £100, we may just settle it to keep the job moving. This is up to you to decide. If it's a larger amount because you are buying a larger, newer house, then speak to the vendors and say that it needs paying if they wish to continue, so please can they pay for it? If they are sensible, they will think that to pull out at this stage, go through the viewing process again, find another buyer in the right position, and start the whole process again is probably not worth it (especially if it's a probate property or has been on the market a long time).

Telegraphic Transfer Fee – £25-£50

When you are transferring deposits, and your solicitors need to transfer the money to the seller's solicitors, you will need to pay for the privilege of sending the money. This is also the same when your solicitor receives the money from your lender. The fees are not huge, but they all add up.

SDLT - £0….All Dependent On Property Value

This is the tax you pay to buy a property, and it's by far the fee I hate to pay the most. When the government announced that they would yet again increase SDLT, and it would start at midnight that night it made me laugh how easily they can push things through when they want to. At the time of writing, it's currently a 3% surcharge up to £125k on the normal SDLT rate if you are buying a 2nd property. So if you are buying a property at £100k, it's a £5k SDLT fee. You then pay a higher rate for the amount the property is over £125'001, so if the property is £150k, it's £8k because you will pay £6'250 SDLT on the £125k, then an additional £1'750 on the amount from £125001-£150'000. Not taking into consideration the refurbishment, but this has always been the biggest '*what am I actually getting for my money*' cost/fee when investing in property. Please research the actual SDLT rates at the time of reading because they may have changed.

Holding Costs

When you have taken ownership of the property, it's very likely you will need to pay for council tax and standing utility charges, etc. So take meter readings as soon as you get the keys, and then contact the providers, saying you are the new owner and you are not responsible for anything before that date. Take pictures of the meters and save them on your computer/cloud. This is best practice for all properties you purchase. Our local council does not give any discount, even if the property has a back-to-brick refurb, and there is no running water. At the end of month 3 and the start of month 4, the council tax is 125% of the normal rate. One of my earliest mentees told me that in his area, if the property has been empty for more than 6 months prior to their purchase, the council tax is 125% from day 1.

Cost Of Finance: Mortgage And Bridging Fees

I'm not going to go into great depth here because the fees you incur will be in relation to the Bank of England base rate, product fees, arrangement fees, and many other '*because we can*' fees. What I would strongly suggest is that when you first get a mortgage offer, sit down and have a look at the number of fees that are payable. Never get subdued by the headline rate, for example, 4.8% but it's got a £5k product fee and ridiculous early redemption charges. Now you may think, '*Well, the ERC can be as high as they want to be because I have no intention of selling.*' However, don't put yourself in that position because you don't know what's around the corner. I'm not saying avoid mortgages with ERC, but be aware of them and act accordingly, try to derisk as much as possible. Always work out the total cost of borrowing for the 3-5 years, don't just look at the headline rate and think because its low it's a good deal. We provide mentees with templates when they enrol into tbe Black Belt Property Academy and the 'true costs of borrowing' is always a good one.

Selling Fees

If you are selling a property then ofcourse you have estate agent fees to pay, I don't know too much about this because we want to keep hold of our properties forever and for the past 20 years we have not sold 1 property. From speaking to agents though I believe they can range from set fees of £995-£2000 or 1.5-2% of the sale price.

From reading the above you may think there are lots of fees and I would agree there are, but if you are in this for the long term then the fees are just part and parcel of being an investor. Treat them like any business expense. For you to get on the ladder and to reap the rewards of passive income for many years to come, you do need to pay fees. What's the other option? Work for 40 hours a week and trade your time for money, then retire on a fraction of what you used to earn? I don't think so, not for our Black Belt investors.

In Summary

Fees are an unavoidable part of building a successful property portfolio, but they're not your enemy. When planned properly, they simply become the cost of doing business and the gateway to long-term, scalable income. The key is to stay educated, factor every fee into your numbers, and treat your portfolio like the wealth-building business it is.

Chapter 38

Why Planning Is Where Most DIY Investors Lose Money?

Black Belt investors treat planning like profit insurance. Get it wrong, and it can cost you thousands; get it right, and it can unlock game-changing value.

When it comes to property investing, planning is one of those areas that can either massively boost your profits or completely wipe them out. It's easy to get caught up in the excitement of a deal and overlook planning, but ignoring it can cost you thousands, delay your project for months, or even kill the deal altogether.

As an investor, you don't need to become a planning consultant yourself (just as you don't need to be an electrician, plasterer, joiner, etc), but you do need to have a working knowledge of what you can and can't do, especially under Permitted Development (PD) rights.

What Is Permitted Development?

In simple terms, Permitted Development rights allow you to make certain changes to a property without going through full planning permission. These rights apply differently depending on your location and whether any restrictions (like Article 4 directions) are in place.

If there's no Article 4 in place, you may have more flexibility than you think. Here are a few examples of what can be done under PD:

Extensions

- **Single-storey rear extension (terraced/semi-detached):**
  Up to 3 metres deep from the original rear wall.
- **Single-storey rear extension (detached):**
  Up to 4 metres deep.
- **Two-storey rear extensions:**
  Up to 3 metres deep — but you'll need *prior approval.*
- **Loft conversions with dormers:**
  Up to $40m^2$ (terraced/semi) or $50m^2$ (detached).

Conversions & Internal Work

- **Garage conversions (attached garages):**
  Often allowed without full planning.
- **Moving internal non-load-bearing walls:**
  Usually fine under PD.

Change Of Use (With Prior Approval)

- **Commercial to Residential (Class MA):**
  Convert shops, offices, etc. into flats (up to $1,500m^2$).
- **Agricultural to Residential (Class Q):**
  Convert barns or outbuildings.

- **Sui Generis to C3:**

  Some changes (e.g., from takeaways or betting shops) are now possible with prior approval.

Know About Article 4

Some areas have Article 4 directions, which restrict or remove PD rights, especially when it comes to things like converting a house into an HMO. If you're investing in an area with Article 4, you'll need full planning permission for changes that might otherwise fall under PD. If the area is an Article 4 area, it doesn't mean you won't be able to convert to an HMO; it just means you need to apply.

A quick note: Wales is entirely covered by Article 4 for HMO conversions. So don't make assumptions, always check with the local council before making plans.

Use Classes And Change Of Use

Properties are legally classified under different Use Classes, and changing from one class to another can require planning permission:

- C3 – Dwelling house (standard single household property)
- C4 – Small HMO (3–6 unrelated individuals)
- Sui Generis – Larger HMO (7+ people), or uses not covered elsewhere

You can often change from C3 to C4 under PD, unless you're in an Article 4 area. But going from Sui Generis back to C3 (e.g., converting a large HMO to serviced accommodation) may devalue the property and will likely require full planning.

Don't Confuse Planning With Licensing

This is a common mistake among new investors. Planning permission is about the *use* of the property. Licensing is about the *amenities* and safety standards, especially for HMOs.

Some key points to know:

- If your HMO houses 5 or more people from more than one household, it must be licensed.
- A licence lasts 5 years and typically costs £400–£1,200 depending on the council.
- Check the maximum occupancy on the licence, if a landlord says it's licensed for 6, actually read the document. Do not accept their word; we suggest you trust but always verify.
- Minimum room sizes:
    - Single room: 6.51m^2
    - Double room: 10.22m^2

Also, avoid renting HMOs to families or tenants with children, unless you're prepared for safeguarding regulations.

Don't Guess: Ask For Help

Before starting a major refurb or a use-class change, always speak to a local planning consultant or architect. I've been lucky to work with two experts over the past few years: one used to be a council planner for over 15 years, and the other is now a private consultant. You'll naturally meet these types of people once you start investing, just don't try to figure everything out on your own. Leverage other people's knowledge and skills to your benefit.

A good rule of thumb: if someone on the same street has already done what you want to do, there's a higher chance your application will be accepted, but still check.

Also, remember that planning takes time. Don't expect to submit an application on Monday and get approved by Friday. Build time into your project plan and don't base your timelines on best-case scenarios.

Black Belt Tip: Buy Subject To Planning

This is critical! Don't buy and then hope planning gets approved. Make your offer conditional on planning permission. If your plan is to build out or convert the property in any way, don't complete the purchase until planning is secured. The exception to this would be if you had another plan with just as good margins involved.

You can also consider option agreements or delayed completions, which give you control of the property while you seek planning, without taking on all the risk upfront.

In Summary

Planning might feel overwhelming at first, but with a solid grasp of the fundamentals and the support of the right professionals, it becomes far more approachable. It's not just bureaucratic red tape — when done properly, planning can unlock significant value in a property. On the flip side, poor planning can lead to costly mistakes. As with every aspect of property, success comes from thinking ahead, doing your research, and never relying on guesswork.

Chapter 39

Turning Wrecks Into Wealth: Your Refurb Strategy

The more work a property needs, the more money you can make, if you control your refurb, not the other way around.

In my experience, the more work a property needs, the better the sale price we have agreed.

A property we purchased in June 2023, we paid £105k for, but it was originally up for £140k, then reduced to £135k. We spent just over £22k on the refurb and properties on that street within 2-minute walk are going from £150-£200k depending on the condition, its now valued at £170k so it's been a nice deal for us. One of the properties we purchased earlier in the year was up for £99k, and we purchased it for £75k (it was a real mess and needed everything other than a new roof). Others on the street in front and behind this house were selling for £130-£140k. Yes, it needed gutting, but remember that this is often where the profit lies. We have just refinanced, and we have left £12.5k in this deal. Some people think that's a lot, but would you like to put in £12.5k and receive +£300pcm for the next 10-20 years?

Always Start At The Top Of The Property

You need to check that the property is water-tight before you start doing a full renovation. Now again, this depends on knowing a reputable builder or roofer who won't say to you that you need a full new roof put on. I'm reminded of that saying, '*Never ask a barber if you need a haircut*;' the same is true for some trades.

When we purchase a property, we have at least viewed the property once, and so have a good idea of the state of the property and what is likely to need work. Ideally, on the first viewing, you managed to pop your head into the loft and have an idea of the state of the roof. I have been on viewings before when you can see daylight through the roof, and even been on a viewing where a pigeon was in the loft space. Pigeons in the loft isn't that bad, though, because it's a great bargaining tool for a lower purchase price.

Holding Costs

As soon as you take ownership of a property, you become responsible for holding costs, whether or not any work has started. These can add up quickly, so it's important to factor them into your refurbishment budget from day one.

One of the first things you should do is take meter readings and contact the energy suppliers to register the property in your name. Even if you're not using much energy initially, you'll still be liable for standing utility charges from the day you become the legal owner.

Council tax is another key cost. In many areas, including where I invest, there are no concessions for empty or uninhabitable properties, so expect to pay full council tax rates during the refurbishment. These can range from around £160 to £250 per month, so be sure to budget for several months' worth of payments.

You also need to consider finance costs. If you're using bridging finance and the lender hasn't retained all the interest upfront (rare), you'll need to cover monthly interest payments during the refurb. Personally, we prefer it when the lender retains the interest at the beginning, it's one less monthly cost to think about during a phase that already feels like it's all money going out. Black Belt investors see the long plan and realise that it won't all be pay out, and they will be receiving most/all of their money back soon.

It's worth remembering that during refurbishment, the property isn't generating income, this is one of the rare times it's a liability rather than an asset. The more aware and prepared you are for these holding costs, the better you can manage your cash flow throughout the project.

Refurbishment Order

I don't want to go into too much detail here on what each step of the refurbishment should look like because every property is different, and it depends on the level of refurbishment needed. The refurbishment order might change, but if you follow this format, you have an idea of the general order...

1. Strip Out

This, in essence, is getting the house back to the shell

a. Removing kitchen and/or bathrooms
b. Removing carpets, vinyl, laminate, and floor tiles
c. Removing woodwork, i.e., skirting boards, architraves, internal doors, etc

d. Removing radiators

Basically, getting the property back to a shell so you can move forward with your fit-out.

We like full back-to-brick refurbishments when implementing the BRRR strategy because, if done properly, you can pull all or most of your money back out of the deal.

2. Getting A Structural Engineer Into The Property

a. If we are having walls removed and/or chimney breasts and/or an extension. They will create drawings for anything that we are moving/creating
b. This can and should be done as soon as possible. It will take time for them to do their drawings, so get this moving quickly.

3. 1st Fix; Electrics + Plumbing + Carpentry (Inc Plastering)

This is when you start to rebuild the property

a. Electrics: fitting new socket locations, upgrading wiring, and the consumer unit if needed
b. Plumbing: putting new piping in place, ready for the kitchen, bathroom, and radiators. Installing a new boiler. Make sure you have your kitchen measured asap
c. Carpentry: put door frames in before plastering, so that plastering can be brought up to them

d. Fit windows at this stage, but not the front door, because we don't want it to get damaged (materials being brought in and out, and waste removal)
e. Plastering the whole house
f. If floors need levelling, then do it after all plastering has been done

4. Tile Bathroom And Fit Kitchen

a. Don't fit the flooring in the kitchen before the kitchen is fitted (however, some people like to tile the floor and then fit the kitchen). For rentals with a vinyl floor, we leave it until the end of the job.

5. 2nd Fix; Electrics + Plumbing + Carpentry

This is the finishing stages of the works, and it's where the property starts to look like it's coming together.

a. Electrics: light switches, light sockets, etc
b. Plumbing: radiators, boiler, etc
c. Carpentry: architrave and woodwork

6. Flooring

a. Tiles in the kitchen here if you didn't do it before the kitchen fitting
b. Vinyl for the kitchen and bathroom should go ahead during the carpet stage below

c. Put the skirting board on after the laminate flooring is down (better/neater finish)

7. **Decorating Stage**

    a. Make sure there is a mist coat after plastering to see any imperfections in plaster. We use satin on wood, matt on walls

8. **Carpets / Vinyl**

    a. Lay in rooms where we want carpet (never lay these before decorating)

At this stage, the inside should be finished, and the front door should be put on. The builder should be handing back keys for snagging.

9. **Snagging**

    This is where you make sure everything is working correctly, and everything is doing what it's supposed to do.

    a. All doors can open and close properly (might need planing after the carpets)
    b. Kitchen: all cupboards and drawers can open and close properly
    c. All taps work
    d. All electrical sockets work
    e. All light sockets are working

f. If renting – check smoke alarms work
g. All windows open and close properly
h. The toilets flush properly

Everything should be exactly as you want it.

Do not make the final payment to the contractor/builder until all snagging has been done. This should have been arranged at the start of the job. A retainer of 5-10% of the total cost should be more than suitable for your builder. One of our builders, who is very good, asks for nothing until it's all complete. Now that is very rare, but it shows he has good cash management and shows he trusts us. If you find a builder like this, then look after them and pay them immediately upon receipt of their invoice.

10. Externals: Rendering And/Or Facades, And/Or Guttering, And/Or Landscaping.

Don't start these until all inside is done because you want to seal the house, you don't want people from 'outside' going 'inside', they don't need to, close the house off to them.

a. Render if you want it done (can be done earlier in the process)
b. Facias and guttering (can be done earlier in the process)
c. Landscaping (this is dependent on garden access; it might need to be done sooner, so the contractor isn't walking through a newly refurbished house)

Leave externals to the last part of the project

Schedule Of Works

A Schedule of Works (SOW) is essentially a plan outlining what needs to happen on your project, when it needs to happen, and who will be doing it. Being organised with your schedule not only keeps the project on track, but also shows trades that you're in control and serious about the build.

If you're new to refurbishment projects, your first couple of schedules might be quite simple, and that's okay. It's a good idea to work closely with your builder to understand realistic timelines and develop the plan together. This ensures everyone is on the same page from the start.

There are different ways to create and display your schedule. Personally, if we project manage, I like to print it on A3 sheets and stick it up on-site as a clear visual reference for everyone involved. It's especially useful if you're making unannounced visits to check progress; in doing so, you can immediately see whether things are running to plan.

In earlier projects, when I was more hands-on and just getting started, I kept it simple: a rough two-week plan printed on an A4 sheet in landscape. It wasn't pretty, but it worked because I was closely involved and knew where each stage was.

Now, we use spreadsheets for our SOWs, printed out and displayed on-site, which helps maintain structure and clarity across the contractors. If the contractors are tech-savvy, then have a working spreadsheet on Google Drive that all can access. As your experience grows and your projects become more complex, your schedules will likely become more detailed too. It's a great learning curve, especially if you're managing a refurb for the first time.

Track Your Expenses

I understand that we all need to pay tax, but we do not want to pay any more tax than we need to. It's therefore in my best interest to track every single receipt/expense in relation to the refurbishment.

If you are dealing with lots of different trades, then let them know that you want receipts for additional items purchased that were not in the original quote. Save every single receipt and invoice and have a running total of the expenses. When it's time to complete the annual tax accounts, you want to be able to see exactly how much you have spent on refurbishments. It's best practice as well to know how much you have spent on the refurbishment, so you know how much money you have put into the deal, and you can then calculate your ROCE. After refinancing, your ROCE should increase if you have managed to pull some, most, or all of your money out of the deal. The more experienced you become, the higher your ROCE should be.

Let Your Insurance Company Know

When your property is empty, insurers require that you let them know it's unoccupied. Likewise, if you are having building works done, I would tell them. I think most people's experience of insurance companies is a bad one, and they will try to wriggle out of anything, but I would always keep them in the loop. Tell them when building work starts and when it's scheduled to end, and when you are likely to have a tenant in place. As soon as a tenant moves in, make it a priority to call the insurers and let them know it's now occupied.

Remember that the refurb 'end product' should reflect the end user and your exit strategy. For example, if we are looking to let it out, then we need it to be clean, tidy, durable, and reflect the tenant type. If we are looking to flip the property, we want to spend more on the finishing touches that will raise the value of the house (soft close doors, thick work tops, higher level of carpet and laminate, etc). The finish of a house we are looking to lease to a social housing company is vastly different from a house we are looking to break the ceiling price on when we sell.

Inventory

Arrange for an inventory to take place because this is the best condition your property is ever going to be in. Make sure you save the inventory photos. On a side note, when we hand over properties on a 3-5 year lease, we take our own personal inventory that is extremely detailed, i.e., 40 pictures per room. We also take detailed videos of how every door opens and closes properly, how the carpet is brand new, etc.

Refurb Costs

The properties I had previously bought at the start of my journey were all ready to move into and didn't really need anything. I had no contacts in the building trade, so this was the only way I knew how. Since I learned about the BRRR strategy, we have only purchased houses where we can clearly add value.

My Early Days

Carrying out the refurbishment can be a stressful or a stress-free process. I remember the first refurb we did; my head was in complete overload. Looking back, the property only needed a bit of plastering under the stairs and in the kitchen, the overgrown alleyway clearing, and the installation of 2 new windows installing. Since I had never done anything like this, I was well and truly out of my comfort zone. I had all the normal feelings, '*what have I done…what if the builders rips me off because they know I don't know what I'm talking about….what if it costs more than I have…*' etc.

I look back at that refurb and realise it wasn't even a refurb – it was a slight nip and tuck.

Each refurb we have done since then has required more extensive work than the last, but has become more organized and more efficient. You will start to build relationships with trades, and they can guide you through the process. As you progress towards a disciplined Black Belt investor, your deals will become more profitable.

Running order of refurb

1. Strip out the property
2. Fix the roof
3. Configuration
4. 1st fix gas and electricity
5. Plastering
6. Bathroom / Kitchen
7. Carpentry
8. 2nd fix gas and electrics
9. Windows and doors
10. Painting
11. Flooring

12. External works: garden, etc (this will move up the list if the landscaper/gardener has to walk through the house, i.e., a mid terrace with no rear access to the back garden)

The above is not a hard and fast rule, but that is how I would organise my refurbishment. Don't have the landscaper inside the house.

How Much Does It All Cost?

The figures below are approx and, depending on when you are reading this book, may be way out of date. The refurbs we were doing pre-March 2020 (Covid) were a lot cheaper than 2022 onwards.

When you are doing your viewings, make sure you calculate how much the refurb will cost based on your checklist and then add on a 10% contingency for a standard 2-bed terrace. For example, if you think the work will come to £20k, then add on 10% (£2k). It's only when you're ripping out the house that you find hidden jobs. For a 3-bed semi, add a 20% contingency. One of the latest projects we have completed had no live gas to the property and no meter. The same property also had a very old incoming main electricity feed that we needed to organise for replacement. Such issues cost a little more than we had budgeted for.

Best practice would be to record every single expense; having keys cut needs to be recorded, as does spending £25 on a key safe for your trades to get access. Every refurbishment you do should become increasingly refined. Eventually, if you are investing in a similar type of property, you can estimate the refurbishment cost to the nearest £50.

The following are approx guides based on what we have paid for recent refurbs for a standard 2-bed terrace. You may be able to get them cheaper, or you may find they are slightly higher in your investment area, but the figures are there to give you a guideline.

Strip Out: £1,500 - £2,500

Back to brick refurb, including removal of waste

Roof: £4,000 - £5,000
Felt, rafters, batons

Facia/Guttering: £1,250 - £2,000

Plastering: +£200

- £3,500 - £4,500 for skim (3-4mm)
- Approx. £5,000 - £6,000 back to brick (baton, insulation, board, skim), dot and dab (adhesive + skim)
- Typical day rate: £200 - £250 per day
- Tip: On your viewings, tap the plaster to see if it's gone/failed

Electrics: £4,000 - £4,500
New consumer unit, sockets, etc. including fit

GCH/Plumbing: £3,500 - £4,000
New boiler + 10-year guarantee + 5 radiators, including fit

Gas:

- Bringing to the property: approx. £500
- £150 per square meter from the main feed

Bathroom: £2,500 - £3,000
Including fit

Kitchen: £2,500 - £4,000
Negotiate for appliances, etc., including fit

Carpentry: £3,000
£30 per door or £150 per door, etc., including fit

Windows/Doors: £5,000 - £6,000
6 windows + composite front door + PVC back door

Flooring/Tiling: £30 - £50 per square meter
Depending on what is done

Painting: £1,500 - £3,000

Damp: +£500-£15,000

- Depends on type: rising, ingress, or penetrative (for end terrace)
- Long-term solution: render and silicone, etc.
- Some older houses may lack a cavity (single brick)
- Ventilation solutions: air bricks, dehumidifiers in lofts, etc, used in HMOs

Rendering: £130 - £160 per square meter

Gardens:

- Depends on size, scope, and features (e.g., large tree)
- Concrete posts and wooden panels: £150 per panel
- Slabbing: £50 per square meter

Driveway:

- Depends on scope
- £100 - £200 per square meter

Extension: £1,800 - £2,200 per square meter

As you can see, there is quite a bit of swing in the prices because it ultimately depends on the size of the house and your end finish. The highest cost is the fixed labour cost; they will charge the same regardless of whether they are fitting a cheap or a dear kitchen. We pay invoices quite regularly, and the above are very accurate.

I can't comment on staircases and driveways because we have never totally replaced them. Likewise, we have only fitted GCH, not electricity- or heat-source pumps.

Inventory

Once the property is 100% complete, take your own inventory for your records. We also use an inventory company to conduct an official one, but we want to know exactly how the property looked when it was finished. An inventory costs approximately £100 for a 2-bed terrace.

It's in your best interest to bring it in on budget and on time. Every day and week the refurb goes over is a day closer to going over your bridging deadline and a day less rent. You need to change the property from a cash-taking liability to a cash-producing asset asap.

In Summary

Refurbishment is a skill you'll develop over time, so start small and improve with each project. Mistakes are part of the learning curve — the best in any industry make them, but they also learn and refine. While refurbishments can be expensive, especially early on, if you're refinancing, think of it as spending £25k to pull out £40k within a few months potentially. Done properly, a refurb not only boosts the property's value and cash flow potential but also reduces the risk of major maintenance issues in the foreseeable future. Each project will sharpen your process, making you more efficient, confident, and profitable.

Chapter 40

Getting The Best From Builders And Tradespeople

Your success in property investing is only as strong as the team behind you. Stop asking "*how do I do this*?" and start asking "*who can do this for me*?" The right tradespeople won't just save you time and stress, they'll make you money.

For your property investment journey to be successful, you need a strong team. We should have the mindset of '*who*' can do this, not '*how*' I can do this. Having a team of professional tradespeople in your little black book will help you overcome the obstacles of property investing. The more you develop properties, the more you will need to work with reputable builders/contractors.

How Do You Find Good Builders?

Many people use online portals like Checkatrade, MyBuilder, etc. I have had mixed experiences with such portals. A bit of advice would be to read the reviews of the trades that are on there. Personally, I would never go with a builder with 0 reviews. Yes, they may be the best builder in the world, and someone needs to give them a chance, but that doesn't mean it has to be me. If I were to choose, I'd go with someone who has decent reviews, not just 1-3.

Speak to people you know who have had building works done. Ask them if they would have the same person back again to do further work. If the answer is '*no*' or '*well, apart from the first week when they only did 3 hours a day,*' then don't bother.

Listen to word of mouth reviews (don't get this mixed up with '*oh I think my hairdresser's husband is a builder*', that is not a review, that's just them telling you what they do).

Visit your local building merchants, kitchen factory, plumbing warehouse, and ask if they have a list of trades. I did this years ago, and they had a recommended list of people they have used. They were in no way associated with the company, but they were happy enough to put them on a list. I found 1 fantastic trade through this method, which we have used on several projects and which we still use today. As time has passed, he has become increasingly focused on property maintenance and gets things sorted quickly.

Classic Google search '*electricians near me*' – then check out their reviews and website. Not having a website does not mean they are bad, 1 know builders and plumbers who don't even have business cards, their work is just always referrals. So if they don't have a website or Facebook page, then don't necessarily write them off; they might just be 'old school'. If they are always busy months in advance and it's all repeat business and referrals, then why market?

When You Find A Good Contractor, Look After Them?

In the early days back in 2007, we used to simply go with the cheapest, which again was the wrong mindset and a complete false economy. There is truth in the sayings '*buy cheap buy twice*' and '*you get what you pay for*'. If somebody's price is too good to be true, it often will be.

When a contractor sends us the invoice, we ensure it's paid that Friday. We tell them beforehand that we pay invoices on Friday. This is great for your smaller jobs, i.e., £5k or less, but for bigger projects such as dorma conversions and extensions, then a payment structure should be agreed ahead of time. Remember that when they see your number on their phone, they don't want to think '*they never pay – I'm not answering that*', you want them to think '*they are professional and pay us on time every time*'. You must build rapport with good contractors.

Never pay a builder 100% up front. Also, don't agree to pay them £X amount every week; you only agree to pay them £X amount each week based on work that has been carried out. One of my best builders doesn't ask for anything until the job is done. I admire the faith he has in his clients, but I would be a bit skeptical about completing 100% of the job without receiving any payment. For the bigger jobs, you should have all this written in your contract.

Have A Contract

Yes, this can seem a bit over the top for some work you may be having done, i.e., replacing front and back doors. If you are doing work that requires ripping out and replacing kitchen and bathrooms, then I always recommend getting a contract. You may not want to go to the solicitors to get it all signed, but the fact that you have things written down makes it clear for both parties. Things that are in the contract:

- ✓ Their name and their company name
- ✓ Property address
- ✓ List and description of works to be done
- ✓ Start date
- ✓ Length of project (expected end date)
- ✓ Deposit needed
- ✓ Payment instalments
- ✓ Contact parameters

Providing a contract will separate you from other 'landlords' who tend to do things on the back of a cigarette packet. You are a serious Black Belt property investor and not a landlord.

Some Signs Of A Bad Builder

Some of the best trades I have used over the years don't have a website simply because they are always busy and see no need to create one. So if they don't have a website or a social media presence, then don't worry. It tends to be the younger generation, i.e., 35 years and under, that have all the socials up and running.

If their van is about 50 years old and not looked after, ok, 50 years old is an exaggeration, but I think that it reflects on them if they are not taking care of their van. I'm not saying they need to have an expensive van that is within 3 years old, but if they aren't willing to take care of their own equipment, how do you think they will care for your project? Traits of a good builder:

- They keep you updated
- They turn up on time
- They aren't popping to go and get something every day due to a lack of planning
- They work Mondays and Friday afternoons
- They don't go off for breakfast after being there just 1 hour
- A really good sign is that they do a Saturday morning to keep things on track

When you arrange to meet them on site, they arrive when they said they were supposed to. A really good sign for me is that they respect my time.

How Do You Know You Are Not Getting Ripped Off?

Again, word of mouth is great, but when you are starting out, I would contact 3 people and ask them for quotes. I don't base it solely on price. If I feel they are genuine and want to work together moving forward, then I will go with my gut. If they are very '*I can't be bothered with this little job*' then I don't work with them. I definitely do not tell them I have a portfolio because they shouldn't change just because they know there will be more jobs further down the line.

Building A Power Team

The power team can be anybody involved in helping you acquire more properties; it can be your broker, solicitor, estate agent, marketing team member, etc. In this section, though, I'm mainly talking about your power team of tradesmen. You should have the following in your power team:

- Architect
- Structural engineer
- Planning consultant
- General builder
- Property maintenance person *
- Roofer
- Carpenter
- Plumber *
- Kitchen fitter
- Glazier
- Decorator
- Landscaper
- EPC / Inventory company

* You should always have 2 of these in your network because most maintenance issues when renting out your property can be fixed by these 2 trades.

You may find that your general builder will often do windows and doors, but there are, of course, people who only do windows and doors. I would be a bit bothered, though, if the plumber said that he also does landscaping, unless he had a business partner, and that's what they did. Be very wary of people who say they can do everything or they 'have a mate' that does what you are after.

Your architect will also be able to guide you on planning and should really not put anything live on the planning portal unless they are confident it will get through. Building your power team does not happen overnight, so just take 1 step at a time; it's all part of your investing journey.

Refurbishing The Property

Depending on how large the refurbishment is, you may only need 1 trade, i.e., a general property maintenance person. For larger refurbishments, you might need more trades, for instance, a general builder, plumber, electrician, etc.

We advise our mentees to take on a smaller project at first, but again, this is based on their personal circumstances. Taking on a smaller project at first will still be a learning experience, and it will set you up for more detailed projects moving forward.

Maintaining The Property

Now, if you want to be as hands-off as possible, then the managing agent you use will, of course, have contractors they use, so you can just get them to do any work needed. The only thing you need to be aware of is that in addition to the 10% approx managing fee you pay for their services, lots of agents also add a % onto the actual invoice. For example, if the call out and work came to £200, the managing agent might put on an extra 10-20% so you could be paying anywhere from £20 to £40 extra. Now, at first, that might not seem like a lot, but when you start to have multiple properties and the bills can be £1000 upwards, then you are starting to see lots of money slip through your fingers. Your job as a Black Belt investor is to keep as much money as you can without sacrificing too much of your time on the low-value tasks.

In Summary

You may have to kiss a few frogs, but when you find a tradesman that does what they say they are going to do and is professional, then add them to your power team. Do not go with the cheapest, go with the person you feel you can best work with and deliver what you want.

Chapter 41
Maximising Your Property's Value At Revaluation

Your profit isn't made when you sell, it's made when you buy, and realised when you refinance. If you want to pull all your money out, every decision from purchase to presentation must shout value.

The number 1 purpose of the BRRR strategy is so you can pull as much money out of the deal as possible. Some investors are ok leaving in £10,000's, but a high percentage of investors want to pull out as much money as possible. Pulling out your money means:

1) You can reinvest the money into the next property
2) You increase your ROCE
3) You are not leaving £1000's in a deal and missing out on future opportunities, i.e., missed opportunity cost

Getting the valuation, you want is down to several factors. It's not just as simple as *'buy a house, do it up, pull all your money out'*. If it were that easy, everybody would be doing it. Some of the factors that determine how much money you can pull from the deal:

1) Buying at the right price
2) Buying in the right area
3) Bringing your refurb costs in on budget and on time
4) Having the wow factor from the kerb
5) Getting the valuation before tenants move in

The biggest factor is, have you added a substantial amount of value?

During the refurb, you should have had your end user in mind throughout. If it's a family home, then have you designed it with family living in mind, i.e., open plan living, storage space, downstairs WC, nice gardens, etc. Doing a good refurb is not all about having the dearest kitchen and bathroom; it's about the end user and how they will feel living in your property.

I'm a positive man, and on the day of the valuation, be positive, think to yourself, *'why would the valuer not value it at the price we have asked for…this house is brand new…. we've not cut corners'*. I mention it a lot throughout this book, but your Black Belt mindset plays a key role in your investing success, indeed, any success, life, business, and health.

Mr Happy Or Mr Grumpy…

Your valuations can all depend on whether you receive Mr (or Mrs) Happy or Mr (or Mrs) Grumpy. The last valuations we have had, we have done very well apart from 1. The person valued it £20k less than what we had put down. He was a real *'pencil pusher'* and very abrasive. They don't tell you that there, and then their thoughts, but your broker should get the news to you within about 24-48 hours. If you do get a bad valuation, then you don't need to accept it; it's a bit of a kick in the teeth, but just go with a different lender. If you have paid a £300-£450 valuation fee, then it's often hard to do, but this is why you need to do your DD before putting in your offer and carrying out the refurb based on your exit plan. Your broker should not just rely on 1 lender; they should have another 2-3 lenders with similar rates lined up just in case you get downvalued. You just need to hope that the other lender doesn't use the same valuer as the original lender. Whichever mortgage company you choose, they don't have in-house surveyors but outsource it to a surveying company. You could go with another lender who could outsource the survey to the same company that did your previous survey. It's rare, but it's happened to us once. You can, of course, appeal the decision, but I don't think the lender will go against their own valuation officer.

Like all things in business and competition, you can only control what you can control. One of my old Sensei's used to say to me, and I in turn to the 10'000 students I've taught *'you can only control your training – don't 2nd guess what the other guy has been doing*. Basically, just be concerned about the way you are training because you have no control over the other guy (unless it's mind games at press conferences, etc).

I feel the same message is true when it comes to your valuation. We can only control the refurbishment and presentation of the house; we cannot control the market, what comparable house prices have sold for, or what mood the valuer will be in. So, with that in mind, reverse engineer the whole process, asking the question *'how do I smash the ceiling price round here…how do I get the value to say 'wow'…'*. You want the valuer to immediately think *'they've done a good job here'* as soon as they look at your house. Carrying out the correct DD and locking in profit/equity from day 1 is integral to a great valuation.

Before and After Photos

It's best practice to take photos of the property throughout the refurbishment. When we first collect the keys, we do a walk-around video (you may have seen some of these on my YouTube channel). We also take pictures of every room as the refurbishment is taking place. They are not only good to look back on when you realise how much a transformation has occurred, but they also come in handy for a valuation pack. I picked the 'valuation pack' up from 1 of my mentors about 10 years ago, who said providing them with a pack that includes before and after pictures and a list of works (maybe even the schedule of works), and invoices helps the valuer. It doesn't need to be overly designed, just a ring folder with a picture of the front elevation, and then before and after pictures of each room.

In the last 5-6 valuations we have done, the valuer didn't want to see what work had been done. I can see it from both sides. They want to value the property on the day they see it; they don't want to look back in time at what it was like and see the transformation. However, I prefer having the pack there, should they wish to see what we have done, because it should only strengthen the argument that we have added a substantial amount of value and we are professionals.

I wouldn't follow the valuer around the property explaining everything you have done. Just be there before they arrive, be polite, and let them know you are there to answer any questions they may have. Depending on what level you are at, you may want to get a deep clean of the property by a professional cleaning agency. This should help everything really stand out. Again, it's about putting your best foot forward and not blending in; do what you can to get the highest valuation possible.

Staging of the Property

Staging of your property, without a doubt, makes it look better. The prospective tenant, buyers, and valuer get to see the property in its best light. It should release emotions and make them see what it's like to live there. Remember that people tend to buy emotionally rather than rationally. For our 2-bed terrace BRRR's, we have never staged because we invest in areas where the rental market is very hot, but if we were looking to flip a 3-bed semi, then I would invest in staging (build this into your refurb figures). Yes, it's likely to cost £2k-£4k, but could that extra money increase my valuation by £10-£20k? As a Black Belt investor, you need to look at things through a return on investment. If somebody said to you that you could spend £3k on staging but it will increase the value of your property by £10-£15k, meaning you will release between £7.5-£11.25k, then you would be daft not to do it. If you are planning on staging the property, make sure you have budgeted for it during your initial refurbishment.

Comparable's

There is, of course, a limit as to the value of your property. If we bought the worst 2-bed terrace in the worst street of our investment area (we don't buy there) for £90k, there is no way we could expect it to be worth £160k after the refurb unless there is a big upswing in the market (something we can't control). After a refurb, we might be able to get it to £120k, but that would be with a £25k refurb, hence making it a pointless exercise. We like to purchase properties about 20-25% BMV, add value through a decent refurb, and then refinance at a much higher value.

You need to be realistic when finding comparables. In some areas, you may be able to walk just 5 minutes down the road, and the area has dramatically changed. Your comparables are best if they are on the same street or 2-3 streets away, i.e., a 5-minute walk. You can't compare your 2-bed end terrace to a 2-bed apartment. Likewise, you can't compare your 2-bed terrace to a 3 or 4 bed semi, so make sure your comparables are exactly that.

Don't be fooled into thinking you need to invest all over the country (unless this is your strategy); try to stick to 1 investment area so that you know where the good and bad areas are. We have been investing in our town for close to 20 years now, so we know areas we would not touch regardless of how good the deal was. Some investors do like to invest up and down the country because it forces them to be hands-off. I'd suggest investors need to do some serious DD if they are purchasing all over the UK.

Recent Sold Prices

The valuer will only go off the last 6 months sold prices, so if there has been no activity for the past 12 months, you are already on the back foot. If you are investing in common stock properties like 2-bed terrace or 3-bed semis, then these are always in demand, and there should be relevant sold prices.

In Summary

Reverse engineer the whole valuation process. Buy at as low a price as possible, do the best refurb possible whilst remaining in budget, and be positive on the day of the valuation. If you are not happy with 1 valuation, then speak to your broker to organise another 1 with another lender. If you carry out your correct DD, you could pull all or most of your money out doing the BRRR strategy, or make a nice lump of cash if flipping.

Chapter 42

Marketing Your Property – How To Stand Out In Any Market?

Great properties don't sell or rent themselves, they're part of a well-thought-out strategy. Presentation, positioning, and platform selection are just as important as bricks and mortar. This chapter shows you how to market your investment for maximum attention, premium pricing, and minimal voids.

First impressions matter. Many investors focus solely on the interior and leave the exterior as an afterthought, often due to poor budgeting or underestimating garden and driveway costs. But if you want to be a successful investor, kerb appeal isn't optional; it's a must.

The only exception might be if you're leasing to a social housing provider for 3–5 years. But if your property is going on the private rental market or especially if you're flipping, you can't afford to neglect the first impression.

Photos Sell

An iPhone might do the job, but when it comes to flips, spend the money on professional photography. If your goal is top dollar, treat your listing like a brand new product launch. If the budget allows, stage the property, spend £2k on staging to spark a bidding war. It's worth every penny if you want to drive up offers.

Features Vs Benefits

Most listings stick to dry facts: "2-bed terrace" or "3-bed townhouse." But that's not what sells a home; you must highlight benefits, not just features.

"2-bed terrace" becomes: *"Stylish 2-bed home with 10-min commute to the city and top-rated schools nearby."*

The location, lifestyle, and convenience sell/rent properties just as much as spec and finish. All the way throughout the refurb, you should be thinking like your ideal buyer or tenant: What would make this property perfect for them? The key is to not overspend, which is easy to do, but to keep your end user in mind.

Know Your Ideal Tenant Or Buyer

You should have clearly defined your target end-user before you even started the refurb. Are you appealing to families? Young professionals? Students? Each group wants something different, and your marketing should reflect that.

A 3-bed semi appeals to a very different audience than a room in an HMO. Your images, description, and tone of your advert need to match the audience you're speaking to.

Advertise On The Right Platforms

Don't be penny-wise and pound-foolish. Yes, portals like Rightmove, Zoopla, and OnTheMarket can be costly, but they deliver serious enquiries.

If you are looking to break ceiling prices then go with an agent who knows how to sell your house and always negotiate a discount on their fees.

Facebook Marketplace is still worth using, after all, it's free, and although you might get time-wasters, there's always the chance of finding a serious lead.

I once put up an A4 poster in the window back in 2007 with "House to Let" on it. It got no traction, and it reflected a scarcity mindset that ultimately slowed my growth. If I'd just done things properly with those first 3 pre-recession properties, we would be further on in our portfolio. However, we acted, and that's what I urge you to do.

Highlight The Lifestyle

This hasn't always been my personal strategy, but when it matters to the end user, it's powerful. For example:

- Transport hubs are a big player
- Top-rated schools within a 5-minute drive
- Walking distance to gyms, cafes, bars
- Quiet neighbourhoods or city buzz, depending on buyer profile

Remember, you're not just selling a property, you're selling a lifestyle. In sales, emotion wins over logic every time. You need to trigger their emotions because people buy emotionally, not rationally.

Let The Market Talk

If your listing isn't generating interest, don't immediately slash the price. Agents often push for price reductions to close quickly. But it might not be the price; it might just be a few tweaks in the advert that are needed. As a new investor, I can understand why some of our mentees say *'the agent said we need to reduce it, so we reduced it,'* but if you know the market well and realise the price you're offering is realistic, then hold on for more money. Sometimes agents advise you to reduce it by £50pcm, which is £600pa. Yes, it might remain on the market 1 month longer, and you have missed out on a month's rent, but think about the long term.

Instead, tweak the advert copy, change the photos, improve the title, and consider re-listing to push it to the top. We did this recently with one of our properties; the tenant had moved out after being in there for 18 months. The property had a full back-to-brick refurb just 18 months previous, and because the property had not been rented for 4 weeks, they suggested we reduce it to less than what the previous tenant was paying. We kept to the new, increased price of £895, tweaked the advert, and secured a tenant within 2 weeks. Remember that agents can give you advice, but that doesn't mean you need to take it.

If, after a prolonged period of time, interest is still low, then reassess pricing; you don't want to lose too much money.

Bonus Tips, Inject Personality Into Your Marketing

If you're marketing your own properties, maybe use these powerful add-ons:

- Create a walkthrough video, builds trust and filters time-wasters
- Add a QR code on signs or flyers that links to a virtual tour
- Build a 1-page website for the property, include videos, photos, local area info, testimonials

In Summary

You've worked hard to source and refurbish your property; now make sure that effort pays off. Great marketing doesn't just help you rent or sell faster, it helps you do it for more money, with better tenants or buyers, and less stress.

Think of marketing as your final layer of value. Present your property like a product you're proud of. Choose your platforms and agents wisely, write like your reader matters, and always lead with benefits, lifestyle, and trust. If you market smarter than your competition, you'll profit faster and with fewer voids.

PART 6

Holding & Scaling For Long-Term Success

After the refurbishment is complete, your journey as a property investor enters a crucial new stage, the holding phase. This period is all about protecting your investment, optimising cash flow, and preparing for future growth opportunities. If you're renting out the property and holding it for long-term appreciation, understanding how to manage and maximise this phase can significantly impact your overall success and wealth. In this section, you'll learn strategies to maintain your asset, increase its value, and set yourself up for the next profitable move.

Chapter 43

Hold Or Fold? Why Wealthy Investors Rarely Sell?

Real estate is the only asset I know where your debt goes down, your value goes up, and someone else pays the bill.

Why "Never Sell" Isn't Just A Catchphrase?

"Never sell" is a phrase we repeat to mentees regularly.

There is, of course, a time and place for selling. If you're flipping a property with the clear intention of rolling the profits into long-term assets that stay in your portfolio, then that's a strategic move. I have no issue with that, but flipping doesn't build wealth; it releases nice lumps of cash, but those lumps of cash should go to acquiring your own cash-flowing assets.

But my goal and what we teach through the Black Belt Property Academy is to help you build a solid financial fortress around yourself. That kind of wealth doesn't come from quick sales. It comes from owning cash-flowing assets that provide passive income, month in, month out.

Let me take you back to my first-ever property. It was my own home, and I purchased it for £89'950. Three years later, I sold it for £104'000 and thought I'd done incredibly well (I sold as prices were on the way up). It felt like a win at the time.

But just recently, the house next door came up for sale at £140'000 — and it was in a poor, dated condition, probably needing another £20'000 spending on it. That's when it hit me (again). I didn't just miss out on capital appreciation over the time of not owning it. I missed out on 20 years of rental income, two full decades of passive cash flow.

Yes, of course, it wouldn't have been 100% passive; there would have inevitably been voids and maintenance. But at the time I sold, that "profit" probably went into the next investment, which helped. Still, every time I drive past that house, I'm reminded of what I gave up. It's a good little reminder to keep hold of property.

The lesson is simple: stop thinking in terms of quick wins and start thinking like a long-term wealth builder. I didn't become a Black Belt overnight, and I certainly didn't become a 6th degree Black Belt overnight either, in property investing, just like in karate, you need to master the basics because those are the foundations of success. Weak foundations result in everything else being weak.

Flipping Vs Holding: What's The Real Cost?

If you're only ever flipping for lump sums and never retaining assets, then you're simply trading in property. You're operating a high-tax, high-effort business. (unless it's extremely systemised). There's nothing wrong with that if you're clear on your goals, but make no mistake, it's a job, not a wealth strategy.

The main difference between BRRR and flipping is the exit strategy: BRRR ends with a refinance and rental income, while flipping ends with a sale and a one-time profit. My view is that if you've already done all the hard work with the refurb, why not refinance, increase your monthly passive income, and build your long-term wealth?

When you sell, you trigger taxes, lose your future cash flow, and break the compounding effect that property provides over decades. Arguably the greatest ever investors, Warren Buffett and Charlie Munger rarely sell stock, and if they do, it is only to invest in something much more appealing. They buy great companies at a fair price and not the other way around; that is what Black Belt investors also do. When you hold, you're thinking like an investor, not a trader.

Activate The Wealth Flywheel

When you refinance a property, extract equity, and hold onto the asset, you tap into what I call the **Wealth Flywheel**, a system where you recycle your capital into the next deal while keeping the cash flow from the first.

You're not taxed on the refinance money because it's considered (good) debt, and it's debt backed by a growing, appreciating asset that someone else is paying down for you. That's powerful, and you certainly don't get that with stocks.

The more of these properties you hold, the faster your portfolio begins to self-fund and scale. The flywheel starts to spin on its own. You shift from chasing income to owning a machine that builds wealth on autopilot.

If you're reading this book, it's because you want to improve your knowledge, build passive income, and create long-term wealth through property. You want to build a strong financial fortress, and you're in the right place.

But here's what you need to understand: you can't scale a meaningful portfolio if you keep selling your best assets. Sure, you might build up some cash reserves, but being rich is not the same as being wealthy. Rich can be temporary, whereas wealth, built the right way, is generational, and that's what I want to build for my family. I expect you're the same.

Cash is great, but monthly cash flow is freedom. Freedom to do what you want when you want.

It might feel tempting to sell when you see the lump sum on the table. I've been there. But hold your nerve and think about the long-term plan. Master the Buy–Refurb–Refinance–Rent model, and play the long game. Black Belt investors become Black Belts because they think long term, and they are not after the quick win. Your future self and your future family will thank you.

In Summary

If your goal is to build lasting wealth, then holding onto your assets, not flipping them for quick cash, is the path forward. Selling might feel like a win in the moment, but true financial independence comes from building a portfolio that pays you every month, grows in value over time, and funds your future without you having to trade your time for money. Property is one of the few vehicles where you can borrow against a rising asset, have someone else pay off the debt, and keep the cash flow, but only if you resist the urge to sell. Long-term wealth requires long-term thinking.

Chapter 44

Best Practices For Holding Your Property

Successful property investing isn't just about buying right, it's about holding smart. Protect your assets, build systems, and make your money work for you over the long haul.

The following is a very small sample of best practices based on my years of property investing.

Keep Some Money For Maintenance

It is inevitable that maintenance issues will come up. If you have done a good refurbishment, then you have somewhat future-proofed your investment. However, issues still arise. Sometimes you can go months without any voids or maintenance issues, and then within the space of 3 months, you might have some void periods, which should tie in with general maintenance checks, plus larger maintenance issues with your other properties. I'm not saying have a pessimistic mindset, I'm just saying you should have cash in reserves for when things go wrong.

From your monthly rent, I would set up an automatic % that moves to a separate account that you refer to as your maintenance account. Simply contact your bank and ask to set up another simple/basic account. Each month, we transfer the equivalent of £50 per property for maintenance (regardless of whether the property is empty or not). These £50s per month start to add up and you have a nice safety net should the boiler need replacing (£1'000-£1'500 approx.). Good financial sense is not to spend all your 'passive' income.

Touch Base With Agents

Even if you do not have the funds ready to go for your next investment, still regularly touch base with agents to remind them that you are still actively investing. You want to be in their mind when they are thinking of certain properties, i.e., if a 4-bed fully refurbed detached is just about to go on the market, I don't expect agents to contact us. However, if a tired and dated 2-bed terrace or 3-bed semi is about to be listed, I want a call from them. You should continually educate them on your requirements, i.e., you should own a space in their head.

You don't need to go to their office every week, but maybe systemise where you physically go into the office once a month and then send them an email once a month, i.e., 2 weeks apart. That way, you are contacting them 24 times per annum. If you are doing this with 5-10 agents, then something will come of it. You may want to make it a little more frequent and pop in every 3 weeks, and do this with 15-20 agents; the more you put in, the more you get out. The key to running and growing a business is structure and systems.

Remind People You Are Still Investing

In addition to the estate agents, I would systemise sending a text or email to friends and acquaintances, reminding them I'm still investing. Let them know of recent success stories because they might want to invest with you moving forward. Maybe send them a snapshot of your journey, including before and afters, returns your deals have achieved, etc. If you tell 50 people you are still investing, then you will start to get 'leads' from this. Letting your trades know you are actively investing is best practice since they will visit many properties and occasionally speak to tired landlords. If something comes of the introduction, then I would look after the trade by giving them a finder's fee of sorts.

Make Your Money Work For You

Rather than squirrel the money you earn from your portfolio into a savings account where inflation will silently erode it, think about the long game. The most successful investors in the world understand the 8th wonder of the world, *compounding*. You should be thinking of your investment journey as a long-term strategy and not a *'get-rich-quick'* scheme. Remember that Warren Buffett says many people want to get rich quickly, but not many people want to take the get rich slowly path. At the Black Belt Property Academy, we advise mentees not to expand their expenses as their income increases. Of course, treat yourself, but if you start to earn £1,000pcm more, then don't have your expenses grow by £1,000pcm. Some of my martial arts school owner mentees have grown their profit by £10-£15kpcm, and that's a lovely position to be in. I believe there is truth in the saying *'if you can't buy 2 you shouldn't buy 1'* and that we should live well within our means. In any business, and property investing is no different, you want to grow your top line as much as possible and keep your expenses very lean, cut the fat where you can.

The money left over from removing the 10% for voids and maintenance should then be allocated to reinvestment. Here is what I would do if I could turn back time to the first 3 properties I purchased:

Rent = £500 pcm
- Mortgage = £250 pcm
- Building insurance = £20 pcm
Cash flow = £230 pcm
- % into void/maintenance account @ £50
Remaining = £180 pcm
Reinvest amount = £100 pcm

Now £100 might not seem a lot, but it will snowball the bigger your portfolio becomes and the more educated you become. It's no coincidence that when I started investing in mentorship, my portfolio substantially grew; I only wish I had done it sooner. I was being held accountable and being forced to focus on the things that move the needle the most. Yes, as the founder of the Black Belt Property Academy, I would of course believe in the value of mentorship because I know firsthand how it speeds up results and reduces mistakes.

Having 1 property is great if it's cash flowing well. Having 5 properties is better, but having 10 or more is a real game-changer. The more you invest, the more you will benefit from compounding.

Continually Systemise Your Business

Systems build a business. I urge you not to build a noisy job. You should not be the filter that 100% of the decisions go through, having you as a bottleneck in your business is bad. You may think at first, '*well I'm only a 1 man/woman band, so I don't need systems yet*', wrong! You need to start the weekly process of adding and tweaking your systems. If you follow my advice, your portfolio will start to grow, along with your cash flow and wealth. You need to continually assess where your time is being spent. We want our mentees to earn as much money as they can with as few headaches as possible.

Look After Your Best Trades At Christmas

For the trades you have used who answer the phone, who have replied to your emails, who haven't let you down, who do a good job, then strengthen the bond in your power team. Every Christmas, send them a handwritten Christmas card and either give them a hamper for their family, a bottle of whisky, Amazon vouchers, some cash, whatever it is, let them know you appreciate their time and services. Becoming a successful investor requires you to buy properties at the right price, but that's only 1 part of the puzzle; you need the contractors to help you realise your goals. It's no use having secured the best deal ever, but not having anybody reliable you trust to carry out the works.

Always Protect The Downside: Insurance And Fixed Rates

Owning property comes with inherent risks, and smart investors know that success isn't just about chasing upside, it's about limiting downside. Protecting the downside means preparing for what could go wrong before it does. This includes having adequate insurance cover (buildings, landlord, and rent protection), maintaining a healthy cash reserve for unexpected repairs or void periods, and structuring your finances prudently to avoid over-leverage.

From a more strategic standpoint, downside protection is about building resilience into your portfolio so that you're not forced into reactive decisions under pressure. That could mean opting for longer-term fixed-rate debt during low interest rate environments to reduce exposure to rate hikes, or stress-testing your cash flow against conservative scenarios, such as rising maintenance costs, rent reductions, or regulatory shifts. You should also monitor your loan-to-value (LTV) ratios to ensure you're not overexposed, aka overgeared, during market downturns where refinancing may be restricted.

Ultimately, protecting the downside ensures that a single adverse event doesn't threaten your broader strategy. In property investment, capital preservation is just as important as capital growth. As the saying goes: *"If you stay in the game, you can win the game."* Downside protection is how you stay in the game.

In Summary

Smart property investing isn't just about buying well, it's about managing well. The key to long-term success lies in protecting your downside, building reliable systems, and making your income work for you. From maintaining healthy cash reserves and strengthening relationships with agents and tradespeople to reinvesting profits and educating your family on financial principles, these best practices help turn a few good deals into lasting wealth. By thinking long-term, systemising your approach, and prioritising both people and planning, you create a resilient, scalable portfolio that works for you, not the other way around.

Chapter 45

Self-Manage Or Outsource? Making The Right Call

Managing your properties isn't just about saving money; it's about deciding where your time and energy deliver the biggest returns. Knowing when to DIY and when to delegate is key to scaling your property business.

Like most things regarding strategy, I believe the 'self-manage or out-source' question depends on your circumstances and your overall 'why'. Are you looking to be as hands-off as possible because your other business is your main focus, or are you looking to escape your 9-5 and build a property business that includes you researching, purchasing, renovating, and managing your own properties? There is no right or wrong way because it depends on your situation and your goals.

My Experience

Back in 2007 and up until 2015, we self-managed. If I could turn back time, I would just let a managing agent look after the properties from day 1. I speak to some mentees who say they will manage their own to save the approx. £100pcm. I completely get it. That's what I did, and that's the mentality I had. It was a '*why should I give them 10% of my rent for hardly doing anything*'.

As my Martial Arts School grew, though, I hated my phone ringing more and more, and having tenants call me up to report a non-entity issue used to rub me the wrong way. I remember a tenant calling me on Christmas Eve, telling me the central heating wasn't working properly – of course, she was 100% right to do so, and it's not a trivial problem, but at that time, I didn't have any emergency gas cover, so it cost me £100 call out (2008 fees) plus the parts needed. I'm not saying you need to have British Gas (or equivalent) emergency cover, but what I am saying is that from that day on, I used to get anxious when my phone rang with a tenant's name. If you do decide to self-manage, you will find that your patience starts to wear thin, and problems always happen on a weekend or a bank holiday. A little leaky tap rarely popped up on a Monday afternoon. Going back to having a strong power team around you when these issues happen (& they will), being able to call your power team will help resolve the problem.

Self-Managing: The Pros

- ✓ You get to keep 100% of the rent, meaning higher cash flow
- ✓ You learn about property maintenance and the typical issues that arise
- ✓ You get to look into the eyes of the tenant upon viewing and sign-up days

Self-Managing: The Cons

- × You have to keep up to date with government legislation and ensure you are doing the tenancy agreements/set-ups

× You're at the coal face more
× Time is taken up, meaning less time for investment

Outsourcing: The Pros

✓ You stay at arm's length, and the rent drops into your account every month
✓ If there is new tenancy legislation, then your managing agent should roll it all out for you
✓ The time you save from dealing with tenants is time that can be used to complete high-value tasks
✓ If you provide the managing agent with a list of your preferred contractors, they can get on with the maintenance without even getting you involved (again, having a Power Team is key)
✓ You build up relationships with agents who may be able to secure you off-market deals, i.e., when an existing landlord is selling up because they can't be bothered anymore

Outsourcing: The Cons

× You sacrifice 10-12% (+ VAT) of the rent, meaning lower cash flow
× You don't learn anything about the 'day-to-day' management of properties
× When there is a void period, the agent won't be as urgent to get a new tenant in as soon as possible
× The inspections might not happen as often as you'd like, meaning maintenance issues are likely to increase

Common Tenant Issues

Should you choose to self-manage or outsource, there are frequent tenant issues that arise. You will notice that the 80/20 principle is in play here, like most things, 80% of the maintenance problems come from approximately 20% of issues.

- The barrel in the door needs to be changed
- Boiler/heating is not working, often the pressure on the boiler just needs topping up
- Plaster has fallen off because they didn't report the water leak issue sooner, it wouldn't have happened if they had told us about the little water leak beforehand
- Condensation in the kitchen or bathroom, often due to the property not being ventilated well enough
- Silicone around the bath/sinks has failed

As your portfolio grows, you want to spend more and more time on things that shift the profit needle the most in your business. As a property investor that is finding and securing deals. Secondary to that is educating yourself from people further on in their journey than you are.

Creating Your Own Management Agency

At the moment, we have just 1 property that we 'self-manage'. This is a property a couple has lived in for over 10 years; they are brilliant tenants, and the house is really looked after. However, as soon as they vacate, I will be doing a little freshening up, refinancing, and then it will be outsourced.

Many investors want to keep the 10% rent that managing agents keep, because when you have a sizeable portfolio (approx. 10 or more), those 10% reductions every month add up and it becomes more appropriate to start your own agency. This does not mean you need to go out and buy or rent a shop front. You can outsource most of it, which means you will still be paying something to manage the properties, but the money is staying within your ecosystem. You might want to do what my wife and I did, which was to set up another company, and she runs the management, but obviously takes a wage from the business each month. We get to see how the portfolio is doing, plus also keep the money floating around us instead of straight out the door.

If I were starting out again, I would make sure that the deal still worked with the 10% management fees taken out. For example:

PP = £100k

Deposit = £25k

SDLT = £5k

Legals = £2k

Mortgage @75%PP = £75k

@5% interest = £3'750pa

mortgage payment each month = £312.50

Rent = £700pcm

Management fees = 10% of £700 = £70 + vat = £84pcm

Cash Flow = £700 - £312.50 - £84 = £303pcm

ROCE = £303 * 12 / £32k = 11%

Bringing this back to your *why*, you would then decide if this is a good enough investment.

Personally, I would look at the £84pcm and see that as the price I pay for somewhat peace of mind and the ability to concentrate on high value tasks. However, conversely, these £84pcm build up when you have 5-10-20 properties. It's not that as your portfolio becomes bigger, things become easier, you do start to earn more money, but *'Every level has a new devil'*. If your application to enrol in the Black Belt Property Academy is successful, which I hope it is, we will build on your skill set year after year as you progress along your journey. The Kaizen mindset will allow you to keep learning and keep improving.

In Summary

If I were to start out again, I would know exactly what my high-value, profit-achieving tasks were and spend 80% or more of my time there; managing tenants is not a high-value task. If, though, you want to learn the ropes for the first few investments and marginally increase your cash flow each month, allowing you to save up more sooner and quicker, then self-manage. Remember, though, that there are many creative strategies where you don't need to put down your own money. Always look at the bigger picture.

Chapter 46

Property Management Systems That Save Time And Money

Without systems, you don't own a property business - you own a job. Build processes from day one to free your time, scale your portfolio, and turn chaos into cash flow.

The aim is not to be a landlord but to run a successful property business, so build it properly from the start.

If you want to create another noisy job for yourself, then don't create systems. Keep getting up every day and putting out the same fires. Month after month and year after year, you will be busy but not necessarily growing a strong, profitable portfolio.

For anybody who has watched any of my YouTube videos (**Dervish Dervish | Black Belt Property Academy**), read my '*How to Build a Highly Profitable Martial Arts School*' book, or read my blogs, they will know I'm a systems man. I built up a very successful Karate School, probably 1 of the best in the country, that grossed more in 1 month than my competition did in 1 to 2 years. Systems helped me do that, so I am a great believer in their power.

What Are Systems?

Think of them like a recipe for cooking. Having the ingredients is 1 step, but knowing what quantity and what order is the real magic.

Your system is a step-by-step guide on how to complete something in your business. It shouldn't be a 50-page document; the best systems are the shortest, most succinct documents. They waste no time in telling the person completing the system how to do the job accurately and effectively.

If you don't have a systemised business, then you are still self-employed, still trade your time for money, and likely *'own a job'*. I want everybody who enrols in the **Black Belt Property Academy** to build a business that pays predictably and reliably every month – systems allow that to happen

Systems We Have Created

- What properties do we buy?
- What to look for on the viewing?
- How to calculate refurb costs and timelines?
- How to calculate the cash flow and ROCE?
- How to put in an offer with the agent?
- Schedule of works for the refurb?
- How to pay invoices?
- How to track rents and expenses?
- How and when to organise gas safety certificates and EICR certificates?
- How to answer the phone?
- How to leave a voicemail?
- How to save contact details?

Plus, much more.

The above is only a small sample. I don't want you to feel you need to complete every possible system because you will end up in analysis paralysis.

When Do I Start?

Yesterday. Don't think to yourself, '*oh, I haven't got any properties yet….I will start systems when I have 5*'. You should start building systems when you are hands-on with building your business. The smaller you are, the better, because you don't have to fit the systems retrospectively.

If you don't have systems, you will prevent your business from growing into something it can be. Systems are what will allow your first team member or VA to take over your lower-value tasks while you concentrate on the higher-value tasks in your business. To grow a successful business, you need people; you can't do it all on your own.

How Do You Create A System?

Create the title, which should be self-explanatory, i.e., '*How To Calculate Refurb Costs?*

A little paragraph under the title explaining what this system is for. Then provide step-by-step guides on how to complete the steps.

In Summary

Systems are often thought of as an unnecessary task because creating them takes you away from doing the business. However, for serious business owners, creating and refining systems is a high-value task. Creating systems means you are working *on* the business and not *in* the business.

Chapter 47

Scaling Without Sinking: How To Grow Without Going Bust?

Scaling your property portfolio isn't about how fast you grow, it's about growing smart, staying solvent, and building a business that lasts beyond the next deal.

As you gain more experience and confidence in property investing, you'll likely want to grow your portfolio, and with good reason. Bigger portfolios mean increased cash flow, greater capital appreciation, and more long-term wealth. But if you want to scale safely, you must understand what comes next. This chapter is about navigating those next levels without losing your footing.

In the early days, you'll likely face at least one of the following: lack of capital, lack of a solid network, or buying in the wrong area. You'll make mistakes & that's part of the process. The key is learning from them and moving on quickly.

When you hit the next stage, where things start to feel like they're gaining momentum, you may feel the urge to scale fast. That's where many investors get caught out. I've seen people go above 80% LTV in pursuit of more deals. Personally, I recommend my mentees stay around 60–65% LTV at this stage. With more properties comes more voids and more maintenance, it's just part and parcel of the game. Smart investors accept this and keep growing, but in a way that's systemised and sustainable.

At higher levels, you're more sensitive to interest rate shifts. A 0.5% or 1% rise might not have bothered you with two properties, but with 12 or 20, it can have a big effect on your monthly cash flow. As with any business, the bigger it gets, the more compliance, vision, and team management are required. We want all our mentees to have a portfolio as big as they want, but we need to remember that at new levels, there are new devils we need to overcome.

Leverage: A Double-Edged Sword

Leverage is a powerful tool, but only if you respect it. Overleveraging is one of the most common reasons investors get burned.

I remember a friend back in the 2000s getting a 110% mortgage. He literally got money *paid* into his account for buying a house. No deposit, no skin in the game. This was peak madness. Maybe you've heard of 'NINJA' mortgages; No Income, No Job or Assets, and yet people were still approved. It was like buying a property was easier than buying bread. When it gets that easy to lend large amounts of money, there is a problem.

You do not want to be in a situation where everything looks great *unless* one tenant moves out or one boiler breaks. I remember having five properties, all tenanted and ticking along nicely, until one property went empty and needed holding costs covered, and another needed a boiler. That nice cash flow? Gone for a few months.

Build A Buffer

You must have a cash buffer. People always ask me, "*How much should I keep aside?*" and the answer is, it depends.

If you have 1–3 properties, then having six months' worth of mortgage payments per property is a good place to start. But if you have 10 or 15 properties, six months' worth across the whole portfolio becomes a significant chunk of cash, money that could be working harder elsewhere.

There's no fixed rule, but I always recommend mentees keep a separate reserve per property they control. It might sit in a business savings account or be offset against a mortgage, but it needs to be accessible if things go wrong, and eventually, something will.

Reducing Risk

As your monthly cash flow grows, you must make it a habit to reduce risk where possible.

Some investors swear by rent guarantee insurance while others think it's a waste of money. It's your call, just make sure your buildings (and contents, should you provide furniture) insurance is solid. Make sure your properties are correctly declared as occupied or unoccupied, depending on their state. These little details can save you tens of thousands if something goes wrong.

Stress-Test Every Deal

No deal is better than a bad deal.

You must always stress test your deals, even if the current interest rate for a 5-year fixed is 5%, we run the numbers at 5.5-6.5%. If the deal doesn't work at the higher rate, we don't do it. Simple.

Likewise, plan for early tenant exits, holding costs, and refurb overruns. If you're doing your first BTL or BRRR, budget for extras. Always, set aside a small emergency fund for every deal. That *"bad tenant"* fund can save your sanity.

Always Use Professionals

Please don't download your lease option agreement from some Facebook group. Use proper professionals, those who are experienced in that particular area. Don't step over pounds to pick up pennies; employ professionals to do a proper job.

Get your agreements checked and work with people who know what they're doing. As your portfolio grows, start building out your power team, mortgage broker, accountant, solicitor, builder, letting agent, etc.

When I was building my Karate school, it was hard for me to hand over responsibility, because I knew no one would do it as well as I. I was a terrible micro-manager. But if you want to grow, you need a team. That's true in martial arts, and it's true in property.

Diversify (But Not Too Soon)

At the beginning, stick to one strategy. Master BRRR, BTL, or HMOs, don't jump around. Avoid "shiny penny syndrome."

Once your foundation is solid, you can diversify. Maybe after 5-6 BTLs, you want to explore HMOs. Great, maybe later you can add Serviced Accommodation to your portfolio. That's smart, and now you're spreading your risk while staying within your lane.

Remember, you're still a property investor, just one with multiple tools in your toolkit.

Grow At Your Pace

Most of our mentees want to grow, and that's great; that's what the Black Belt Property Academy is for. But you need to plan your growth, not just chase growth for growth's sake. You must grow based on your timeline and goals, not from looking at some influencer.

One deal with great margins is better than four stressful ones with poor returns. Don't fall for the social media hype, Lamborghinis and *"£10K per month from property in 30 days"* screenshots aren't the goal.

Comparison is the thief of joy. If you're happy doing one deal a year for the next 10 years, that's brilliant. You'll still end up with more properties than 99% of people. If you want to go faster, that's great too. Just make sure it's *your* decision, not someone else's Instagram highlight reel.

In Summary

Scaling your property portfolio should be exciting, but never reckless. Leverage wisely, build a cash buffer, stress test every deal, and work with professionals. Diversify your strategies once you've mastered one, and never compare your journey to someone else's. Grow with intention, protect your downside, and you'll build a property business that not only thrives, but lasts.

Chapter 48

When And How To Refinance For Long-Term Growth?

Refinancing is not a cash grab. It's a strategic lever to recycle equity, accelerate growth, and build lasting wealth without risking your cash flow.

Rule Number 1 Of Refinancing

Don't pull money out of a cash-producing asset to go and buy a liability.

You can ignore that rule, but that's how people undo all the hard work they've put in.

Refinancing should be a strategic move to release trapped equity that can help fund your next investment. When done properly, refinancing can accelerate your journey, but if done without planning, it can harm your cash flow and long-term wealth.

Timing Is Everything

If you've bought at a low enough price and added value through a well-planned refurb, then you've earned the right to refinance. Just make sure it's at a level you feel comfortable with, and the proceeds move on to your next investment.

There's an unwritten *"6-month rule"* in the industry. Most lenders won't allow you to refinance if you've owned the property for less than six months, so always plan accordingly. A refurb that we finished earlier this year was finished just after 4 months. We could not access the refinance money, but we worked with the solicitors to ensure we could complete at exactly the 6-month point of ownership.

In BRRR, I like to switch the final two R's; we refinance *before* renting. Yes, you might lose a month or two of rental income, but you'll likely gain a stronger valuation. You want the valuer to walk into a perfectly presented property. If you've already moved a tenant in, they could be messy or even confrontational, and that will likely harm your valuation.

Think long-term: don't step over pounds to pick up pennies.

Why Refinance?

If you're serious about building a portfolio, you'll need to recycle your money. Most investors don't have an unlimited pot, and even if you're working with joint venture partners, BRRR allows you to keep momentum.

At the time of refinancing, you may even secure better mortgage rates than when you originally bought. This can improve cash flow, but often, you'll pull equity out at the cost of slightly lower monthly profit. That trade-off is worth it if it gets you into your next deal, where you will benefit from capital growth and a new passive income stream. Investors who don't refinance solely based on the reduction of the cash flow they receive are thinking too short-term.

What If You're Down Valued?

If your valuation comes back lower than expected, speak to your broker immediately. Ask them to find another lender, even if the rates aren't quite as competitive, you might still be able to release the funds you need.

Always aim slightly higher on your valuation. Last year, we submitted a figure of £160k, even though we thought £150k was more likely. The valuer agreed at £160k, and that extra £7.5k went straight into our next project. Well, it should have done, but it got gobbled up with some extensive dampwork on another property; these things happen.

Just remember: some down valuations are out of your control. If you've done a solid refurb and know you've added value, you've done your part. You might just have had a "*Mr Grumpy*" valuer; we've had a few. Don't waste time arguing or appealing. Just get back on the phone with your broker and change lenders.

What If You Leave Some Money In?

In an ideal world, you'd pull all your money out, maybe even extra. But often you'll need to leave a bit in.

Let's say you leave £10k in the deal and you're earning £300pcm net. That's a 36% return on capital employed, better than most investments out there.

But if you're leaving £25k in a £120k property, that's a sign something went wrong in the deal. You need to be able to recognise the difference, and it starts with education. Being able to pull out as much money as possible from your projects is a learned skill that comes with time and practice. The rewards are there if you are willing to make mistakes and fail a few times.

Know Your Exit Before You Enter

Before viewing a property, you should already know your numbers. It's not enough to think it's *"a good price."* You must:

- ✓ Spot where you can add value
- ✓ Know as accurately as possible the end value post-refurb
- ✓ Ensure the uplift covers refurb, holding costs, SDLT, and still gives you equity to pull out

Without that clarity, you're just guessing, and guessing leads to losing money.

Your Broker Is Key

A good broker is part of your power team. They'll guide you through bridging loans, long-term finance, and make sure your strategy is aligned with your exit.

But they can't read your mind, you need to tell them if this is a BRRR, if you're refinancing quickly, or if it's a long-term hold. You need to let them know so they can find the product that best suits your needs.

Compounding Is The 8th Wonder

You need to have the correct mindset and understand that if you pull £25k from one deal and reinvest it, you could double its value over the next 10–15 years. Following the property cycle, we both know that the property will increase in value over the long term.

This is why I always say: *don't blow your first few refinances on liabilities* if you want to buy the flashy car, fine, but do it when your cash flow can easily cover the payments without blinking.

Let your money compound, and it will build you wealth beyond what you can imagine.

What About Tax?

Always seek professional advice, but the good news is that there's currently no tax on refinancing because it's not income; it's debt. You're increasing your debt, not realizing a profit. That could change in the future, so make sure you're working with an accountant who understands your strategy.

When Not To Refinance?

Just because you can refinance doesn't mean you should. If your portfolio is ticking over nicely and you're comfortable with the cash flow, it might make sense to leave the equity in and keep your LTV low.

We personally aim for around 50% LTV in later life. We don't plan to pay off everything, inflation will erode the debt over time, but we want a safe, stress-free portfolio when we're older.

In Summary

Refinancing is a powerful tool, but only when used strategically. It's not free money; it's an opportunity to grow your wealth if you're disciplined. Know your numbers, build your team, and always refinance with purpose. Don't cash in your equity to fund liabilities, reinvest it into income-generating assets and let compounding work its magic.

Chapter 49

Ready To Grow?

Here's How To Get Started

Congratulations! Most people never finish a book. By reading this far, you've shown you're serious about creating real change in your life.

But knowledge alone isn't enough. Reading is the first step, but applied knowledge is what transforms results. It's time to turn what you've learned into tangible growth: better cash flow, passive income, and long-term wealth.

If you're ready to take your property journey to the next level, the **Black Belt Property Accelerator** is the next logical step. The Accelerator isn't a generic course. It's a mentorship program designed to prepare you for the Academy where you are taught to think and act like a disciplined investor.

I've been investing since 2007, building an income-producing portfolio using BRRR, BTL, and HMO strategies, while running one of the UK's most successful martial arts schools. The same discipline, focus, and structured learning that helped my students earn their Black Belts is embedded in every aspect of this mentorship.

Whether you're just starting out or looking to scale, here's what we help you achieve:

- Build and grow a sustainable property business

- Avoid the costly mistakes most investors make
- Think, act, and invest like a professional
- Navigate challenges with confidence
- Achieve financial freedom

This is not a sales pitch, it's an invitation to explore whether this mentorship is the right fit for you. If it feels aligned, you can take your first step today.

Scan the QR code below or visit **DervishDervish.com** to learn more and apply.

Let's build something meaningful together.

Dervish Dervish

Founder, **Black Belt Property Academy**

6th Degree Black Belt | Author | BSc | PGCE

Inside The Black Belt Property Academy

Real-World mentorship for investors ready to transform their lives

Property investing requires **discipline, structure, and precision,** the same principles I've coached for decades as a 6th Dan Black Belt. Inside the Black Belt Property Academy, I teach investors to master property the same way a martial artist earns their Black Belt: with clarity, focus, and an understanding that each weekly lesson brings you closer to your goal.

I've been investing since 2007, completing dozens of deals (BRRRs, BTLs & HMOs). I've made mistakes, learned the lessons, and built a profitable portfolio that now funds the life I want.

But this Academy is about more than property. I've also run a successful martial arts school for decades, coaching hundreds of students to earn their Black Belts. The same philosophy of discipline, structure, and progressive mastery guides every step in the Academy.

Inside the Academy, you go from being a White Belt Beginner to a **Confident Black Belt Investor.** Someone who can source, fund, grow, and scale with confidence, strategy, and skill.

What Makes The Academy Different?

We are not just another course provider. This isn't hype, theory, or motivational fluff. It's real-world, step-by-step mentorship that meets you where you are and takes you further than you thought possible.

Students in the Academy consistently:

- ✓ Secure their first (or next) profitable deal
- ✓ Avoid mistakes amateurs make
- ✓ Build confidence in decision-making
- ✓ Learn systems for growth and scaling
- ✓ Benefit from a structured martial arts-style progression

Whether you're just starting out or already have a few deals under your belt, the Academy is designed to help you **grow your portfolio with precision and develop as an investor.**

What You Can Expect When You Enrol?

- ✓ A **clear, structured path** to building a profitable property business
- ✓ High-accountability support
- ✓ Training built by a **qualified lecturer**, breaking complex topics into actionable steps
- ✓ Focus on **mindset, strategy, and execution**, not just tactics
- ✓ A community where disciplined execution and strategic thinking are standard
- ✓ Tailored tiers for starting or scaling investors
- ✓ Celebration of each "belt promotion" you achieve on your journey

Your Transformation Inside The Academy

This is where theory becomes momentum, and momentum becomes **financial freedom.**

- ✓ Investors who follow the Black Belt framework consistently make decisions with clarity and discipline
- ✓ Move from scattered knowledge to real-world implementation
- ✓ Be surrounded by action-takers, not lone wolves
- ✓ Transition from *"Can I do this?"* to *"Here's my next move"*

Take The Next Step

If this resonates with you and you're ready to turn knowledge into action, the Black Belt Property Academy is where you **make it happen**. If the Black Belt approach resonates with your goals, explore how the Academy's structured progression can support your journey. Enrolment is based on alignment and readiness.

Scan the QR code and let's take the first step together.

Check out my YouTube channel for educational videos:

YouTube: Dervish Dervish | Black Belt Property Academy

PART 7

Bonus Lessons, Mistakes, And Action Steps

Success in property isn't just about strategy; it's about staying the course, learning from experience, and taking bold action. In this final section, I'll share the biggest lessons I've learned (often the hard way), answer key questions like whether to pay off your mortgage early, and show you how the right mindset and mentorship can dramatically accelerate your journey. Wherever you're starting from, what matters now is what you do next because knowledge is only power when you act on it

Bonus: 1

10 Mistakes That Cost Me Time, Money, And Sleep

Since 2007, I have made some very big mistakes. The most successful investors I know with +200 properties have made lots of mistakes. What separates them from other investors who have 1-2 properties is that they could see the bigger picture, learned from their mistakes, and kept going.

Anybody new to the property investing world, reading this, I genuinely wish you all the best, and hopefully, this book has gone some way in helping you on your journey. Please take on board my top 10 points below, please learn from my mistakes & learn from other people's mistakes too. The more you learn, the more you earn, so don't stop learning.

For those of you who have a mentor, I urge you to not only ask for their advice and guidance but also ask them about the mistakes they have made. I feel we can learn more from mistakes than successes because they prevent us from pushing our success back. Success isn't a great teacher, but failure is. I openly share my mistakes with my mentees and students; I believe it shows transparency and shows that I'm human. I used to teach Karate 6 days a week, and I would always let the higher grades know of mistakes I made in my training – mistakes that led to me being swept during sparring and ending up on my backside! The property equivalent is overpaying for a property, spending too much on a refurb, not being able to pull as much money out as you'd like, void periods, plus many more.

Here we go, my top 10 biggest mistakes:

1. **I just used to offer the asking price**: I used to see how much the property was marketed for in the newspaper (yes, that's how old I am), and then if I liked it on the viewing, I'd say something stupid like '*yes, I'll have it*'. Imagine how much I've overpaid for properties by not even negotiating!!! What an amateur – estate agents must have loved me. Now is not the time to go into negotiation tactics, but if you do negotiate, never meet halfway, ever! Have a maximum price you will pay and make sure that's demonstrated on your 3rd and final offer. Never, ever, exceed your 3rd and last offer.

2. **Price shopping when it comes to solicitors**: Going with the cheapest, even though they were slow and unprofessional (like a sausage factory). I say this a lot, but most times, '*you get what you pay for*'. If a particular solicitor is considerably cheaper than others, then there will be a reason why. They will take on that many clients to make up their profits, and as a result, the care will be bad. I suggest staying away from online only solicitors.

3. **Using the cheapest trades**: I thought this was good, saving £20 here and there, picking up the materials myself, going to the skip with rubbish, but in theory it was a false economy, as I say above, '*you get what you pay for*'. Driving to the merchants or going to the skip to get rid of rubbish is not the best use of your time. Seek 3 quotes and then decide. At that time though, I had no idea about low-value tasks and high-value tasks. I was just happy being a busy fool. One of the distinctions I see with my mentees is that those

who value their time achieve greater success and start to realise their true worth.

4. **I didn't do thorough reference checks**: My checks back in the day were as detailed as *'have you got a pulse'* and that was it. If they could move in within 2-3 days, that fastracked them – big mistake! Not doing proper reference checks means you could get a tenant in who doesn't pay the rent, and then you have to evict. I have had 2 tenants do a midnight bunk owing me rent, and both tenants I didn't do any reference checks on. Don't skip correct DD on vetting your tenants. Yes, it can not be 100% foolproof, but it's a good start.

5. **I'd fall for all types of rent excuses**: They hadn't been paid, their partner hadn't transferred their money, there was no overtime at work, they spent it on a night out, it was their child's birthday, it's January, and they didn't have money for rent!! Meanwhile, they always had money for cigarettes and alcohol. The rent coming in on time every month is part of the agreement, so get this right from day 1.

6. **I didn't reinvest back into the property**: I would delay jobs for as long as possible, rather than getting them fixed asap. At the end of the day, it's my property, so I should preserve it. If I want it to keep providing me money every month for the rest of my life, then I need to look after it. Problems do not fix themselves; as soon as a maintenance issue is reported, start the process of fixing it. Doing so also shows the tenant you are professional.

7. **Not having a proper plan**: My plan was to just buy cheap houses and rent them out, that's it, I wasn't bothered about the area or tenant demand. I, of course, was uneducated, so my plan was just to try and make some money each month from the properties, that's it. There was no generational planning, BRRR knowledge, and definitely no Kaizen mindset. All I knew was single lets, I knew nothing of SA, HMOs, title splits, etc. Serious investors have plans.

8. **Using all my own money**: This limits the size of your portfolio. I'm sure that if you had £10million in the bank, you would still run out of money if you keep dropping 25% deposits and carrying out extensive refurbishments. Tell and show people what you do, and that you can pay them more interest than the banks, and people will eventually ask you questions about how they can be part of it.

9. **I stopped investing in 2008 for a few years**: Think of all the profit I could have locked in purchasing when property was being sold cheaply, post-financial crash! I was convinced that the property market would never pick up, and I was just unlucky (another sign of lack of education). I therefore took this time to build up my full-time Karate school. In hindsight, I should have continued to purchase even if it was just 1 property a year. If I had done that, the properties would now be worth double what I paid for them. Hindsight is a brilliant thing. Do not stop investing. You may choose to slow down at some point, but I wouldn't recommend stopping.

10. **THE BIGGEST ONE…….I did not educate myself**: Knowledge is power, but 1 thing I tell my mentees across all levels (Accelerator – Academy – Mastermind – Inner Circle) is that applied knowledge is power. If I knew then what I know now, I would have a much larger and more profitable portfolio. I had no plan and no mentor to highlight pitfalls and map the journey for me. I was humble but thought, '*How hard can it be?*' Just buy a house and put a tenant in it, watch the money come in. Wrong! There is no doubt in my mind that if I didn't have that scarcity mindset and I had a mentor, my portfolio would probably be double, maybe triple the size it is now. As soon as I invested in a martial arts business mentor, my single school doubled and tripled in income. The same happened when I invested in a property mentor; my portfolio grew more in 3 years than it had in the previous 10.

I don't regret making the above mistakes because ultimately, they have taught me to be a better investor, and as a result, I have reaped rewards from my property investing journey. Making these mistakes allows me to pass them on to my mentees, which in turn helps them become better. There are lots more mistakes I have made, but the above 10 are the most important, I believe, for new investors.

Bonus: 2

5 Traits Of Successful Black Belt Property Investors

Property investing looks easy from the outside; most things do from the outside when you are watching professionals. But as you'll know by now, success requires more than just a deposit and a good postcode. You need to be educated to achieve great results.

Over the years, I've worked with hundreds of people from martial arts students to full-time investors, and the ones who rise to the top all have a few things in common.

Here are the 5 traits that separate the dreamers from the doers.

Trait 1: Action Over Analysis

The best investors don't wait until every variable is perfect; they take informed action. They do not wait for all the traffic lights to turn green because they realise they won't go anywhere. They run the numbers, consult the right people, and get moving.

You don't need to know every step of the journey before you take the first one; you just need to start.

✓ What This Looks Like?

- Viewing properties before they feel 100% ready

- Making offers with solid due diligence
- Learning by doing, not just reading

Trait 2: Resilience When It Gets Tough

Every investor hits a wall. Builders ghost you, refurbs go over budget, deals fall through, valuations come back low, completion deadlines get pushed back, etc.

What separates successful investors is their ability to keep going, solve problems, and come back smarter. They show '*Black Belt Perseverance*' – one thing we build in all our mentees.

Your mindset is the real asset, not the property.

✓ **What This Looks Like?**

- Staying calm during delays
- Not giving up after one bad deal
- Learning from mistakes, not blaming the market

Trait 3: Obsession With The Numbers

Forget Instagram renovations and 'check me out' videos, the winners focus on spreadsheets more than splashbacks. They know exactly what makes a deal work before they commit. They are meticulous with the important numbers.

✓ **What This Looks Like?**

- ROCE, cash flow, yield — always top of mind
- Cost control and budget planning

- Refusing to fudge the figures to justify a deal

Trait 4: Coachability & Humility

Great investors don't try to reinvent the wheel. They seek guidance, follow proven frameworks, and don't let ego get in the way of growth. Follow Success and Success Follows. You can go fast alone, but you'll go further with the right mentor.

✓ **What This Looks Like?**

- Asking for advice
- Learning from others' mistakes
- Admitting when they don't know something and fixing it fast

Trait 5: Delayed Gratification

The best investors aren't chasing Lambo's after Deal #1. I do like nice cars, but I waited until I could easily afford them. The Black Belt investors are playing the long game; they're using cash flow and equity to build wealth, not to show off.

Wealth is what you don't see, the assets, not the accessories.

✓ **What This Looks Like?**

- Reinvesting profits
- Living below their means to grow faster
- Letting compounding do the heavy lifting over time

If you recognise these traits in yourself, or want to develop them, you're already ahead of the game. These are the exact principles we build into the Black Belt Property Academy.

With the right guidance, environment, and support, you can go from white belt beginner to Black Belt expert faster than you think.

Bonus 3

Should You Pay Off Your Mortgage Early?

This depends! If you are looking to own only 1 property, then, of course, pay it off so you reduce your outgoings each month. However, reading below may make you think otherwise.

As a property investor, I am in no rush to pay off the mortgages I have on our investment portfolio. We are in it for the long haul and understand inflation will erode the debt every year we own the property.

Maybe like you, I was brought up to try hard at school, get good grades, get a good job, work hard, save up, and pay off your mortgage. There are worse ways to grow up, but this is not how to become wealthy. It's a good way to become 'comfy,' but I'm sure you want more than just to be comfy. One thing to remember is that you cannot save your way to wealth; you invest your way to wealth.

If you had £100k in the bank and your own mortgage was £100k, then you could pay it off so that you didn't have any more mortgage payments each month. Having that extra £500 pcm mortgage payment not debited from your account would be nice. Or another option would be to split that £100k into several deposits (depending on your investment area). For easy maths, let us just say you could split it into 4 * £25k deposits and take ownership of 4 properties worth £100k. You have now increased your net wealth, your passive income, and the ROI on your £100k. Yes, you now have 4 mortgages, but this is good debt because it's secured by an appreciating asset that should provide you with positive cash flow most months, and the monthly debt is paid by your tenants.

With my first business, I was lucky to earn a nice amount of money and pay off my mortgage at age 30. I could have written a cheque to settle the entire £101'000 balance, leaving my house unencumbered. £100k may not seem a lot, but it was back in 2012 (that's inflation again). The only reason I did not do this was not because of any superior financial intelligence I had, the complete opposite; it was an ego trip, I liked seeing my bank balance go up every month. I eventually paid off my mortgage at age 33, and it felt great. So many people strive to be 'mortgage-free,' and it is a nice feeling, but because cash flow was not really a problem, the feeling of being mortgage-free lasted a couple of months; it was then just the norm.

Going back to the example above, imagine that in 10 years, the £100k property had increased by 20%, meaning the single house was worth £120k, while the 4 houses had also increased by £20k each, for an overall increase of £80k. Who is in the better position? The person whose net wealth has increased by £20k or the person who has increased by £80k and benefited from positive cash flow for most of that time. You can say that if the person's residential home was worth £300k, then they too have benefited from a £60k uplift, but there has been no monthly cash flow, unlike with the rental properties.

If you are an investor, you need to get comfortable with good debt because that is where you will grow your wealth.

Bonus: 4

Success Doesn't Happen By Accident

If you don't do anything, you'll fail. But if you do something, anything, you have a chance at success. Sitting on the fence delays your growth.

How many people do you know who say they want to get into property investing… but never do?

They've read the books, watched the videos, been to a seminar or two, but nothing ever changes.

No offers are made, no deals are done, and no wealth is created. It's sad, but they just fall back into their normal lives, which they wanted to get out of in the first place.

Let me be brutally honest: Success doesn't come from watching. It comes from doing, doing the right things day in, day out. Just as your property investments compound, so will your success habits.

Your Success Will Be Defined By What You Do Next?

There's a big difference between having goals and taking action. Goals feel good, but action *gets results.*

Here's what action looks like in real life:

- ✓ Go to 3 networking events this month
- ✓ Speak to 3 mortgage brokers
- ✓ Speak to 4 estate agents
- ✓ Book and attend 5 property viewings

- ✓ Post on social media 15-20 times to build visibility and attract investors

These might seem small, but together they build momentum, and momentum is everything in property. You must do things daily to take you closer to where you want to go.

The biggest action I found was committing to becoming better and having somebody hold me accountable. The above action points can easily get pushed to the side but having a weekly property lesson and speaking to a property mentor further ahead than you really improves your chances of success.

Don't Wait Until You "Know It All"

If you're waiting until you've got every strategy memorised before starting, you'll never start. Remember Zig Ziglar's famous quote, '*if you wait for all the traffic lights to turn green, you won't go anywhere*' – that's exactly the property case.

Some of the most successful investors I mentor started with imperfect knowledge, but they took perfect action.

They made offers, ran numbers, booked viewings, and kept showing up. Every time they did, they got that little bit better and took a step closer to their goals.

Clarity comes from action, not overthinking.

You've Already Started, So Don't Stop Now

By buying this book, you've already proven you're serious. You've taken that first step most people never take.

But don't stop here; otherwise, this becomes just another property book on your shelf.

Ask yourself: What will I do this week to take me closer to where I need to get to?

If you don't have an answer, then that's your next priority. Set one now!

This Is Exactly How We Help Our Students

Inside the Black Belt Property Academy, we guide investors to take smart, focused action:

- Find and assess your ideal investment area
- Analyse real deals that stack
- Learn proven negotiation strategies
- Attract Joint Venture partners
- Plan profitable refurbs
- Systemise your business
- Recycle cash through smart refinancing
- Build a leveraged power team
- Save thousands through tax-smart structuring
- Hire a VA and go remote
- Implement a strategy for balance and growth

So What's Your Next Step?

If you're still on the fence, ask yourself:

"What has inaction already cost me?"

Lost time, lost opportunities, financial peace of mind? The cost of inaction is far greater than action, but it's often so small we don't see it. We don't see the weight we are putting on until 1 day we look at a picture of ourselves or try to fit into clothes we haven't worn in a while. In the not-so-distant future somebody you haven't seen for a while will ask, *'How's that property thing going?'* You want to be able to tell them, humbly, about your large portfolio that enables you not to have to work again and keeps your family in a great life.

You don't need to be perfect; you just need to move in the right direction. Every successful investor I know started by deciding to go all in. Every Black Belt I graduated started as a white belt; they became Black Belts because they committed to and kept coming to class. That's the mindset we teach in the Black Belt Property Academy.

Want Help Taking Your First (Or Next) Step?

That's what the **Black Belt Property Accelerator** is for. Check out the information at the back of this book. Success doesn't happen by accident. It happens by intention, by decision, and ultimately by doing.

Bonus: 5

The Best Investment You Can Make Is In Yourself

You've probably heard the saying "*knowledge is power*", but in my opinion, it's applied knowledge that holds the real power.

There are plenty of knowledgeable people who never reach their potential. I'm an avid reader and always working to improve my value, but I'll admit, I haven't always applied everything I've learned either.

So, I urge you: don't just read this book, think "*that was good*," and put it back on the shelf. Revisit it, use it, and let it deepen your knowledge and sharpen your action.

I believe it was Benjamin Franklin who said, *"Empty your purse into your mind."* That wisdom has echoed for centuries, an investment in yourself is the only one that can never be taken away. It offers the best ROI you'll ever get, far better than any property deal.

When I started out in 2007, I knew nothing about the BRRR strategy, yet I've now recycled well over £500'000 using it. I knew nothing about creative finance, HMOs, and SA. Now I use them regularly. I often tell my mentees: *"We don't know what we don't know."* That's true, especially in property.

Every one of us needs someone further along the journey to learn from. When you invest in yourself, you unlock not just knowledge but opportunities worth hundreds of thousands (maybe even millions), depending on your application.

Personally, I've invested over £60'000 in martial arts business mentorships and around £75'000 in property masterminds and coaching. I think that's a lot but I had to push through to achieve the next levels in my business. I think it's what helped me unlock millions. The ROI on that money is infinite; HMRC can't tax it, and it helps me continue to grow our portfolio.

I still remember my first £5,000 course; before then, I was trying to patch everything together, which wasted a lot of time and cost me profits. Friends thought I was mad. But my next deal brought in £20,000, and I've been using those skills ever since.

If this book has resonated with you, the next step is clear. Apply to enrol in the **Black Belt Property Academy,** my proven mentorship programme for investors who want to scale smarter, faster, and with less guesswork. You'll get the tools, accountability, and mindset shifts to level up your income and impact.

And if not with me, keep investing in yourself. Keep learning because if you're struggling to find the time or money to grow, that's the clearest sign that you need to. To be more successful than you are right now, you need to invest in yourself and take action.

The property will pay you, but only when you become the person who can manage the wealth it creates.

Bonus: 6

My First-Ever Investment Property

The Deal That Started It All

Here it is, my very first investment property. It's not flashy, and it's certainly not in the best area of town. It's just a basic 2-up-2-down terrace that most people would have walked straight past. I made many mistakes with this one (and the next two properties). I didn't know anything beyond buying a house and renting it out; that was my very limited property knowledge.

I bought it in 2007, made every beginner mistake possible, and for years after the 2008 financial crash, it sat in negative equity. But even with all that, it still did what property does best when approached with long-term thinking. We have earned passive income from it for about 90% of the time we have owned it, and it has more than doubled in value.

Here are the numbers:

Purchased: £60,000 in 2007 (overpaid!)
Revalued in 2024 at £120,000
Refurbishment cost: £18,000 after 17 years of ownership (= £1000pa)
Rent history

- Originally £350 pcm
- Later increased to £600 pcm
- Current market rent would be £750 pcm
- Now leased at £575 pcm with no maintenance costs and no void periods
- \+ we received a £2'500 grant from the housing provider

Value in 2026: £140,000–£150,000
Total growth: +£80,000, which is 233 % of the original purchase price

Cash flow over the years

- Approximately £200 pcm × 12 months × 10 years = £24,000
- Approximately £300 pcm × 12 months × 5 years = £18,000

Total estimated cash flow: £42,000 (over compensating for 3 years of excessive voids)

This little house, the one that didn't look like anything special, taught me more than any seminar, course, or YouTube video ever could:

- The property doesn't need to be perfect to work
- Time and consistency beat hype and shortcuts
- Small beginnings can lead to big results

That first deal changed my life & if you take action, your first one might do the same for you.

About The Author

Dervish Dervish is a 6th Degree Master Black Belt, property investor, qualified lecturer, and mentor with more than two decades of experience in martial arts, business, and personal development. Trained under and endorsed by Europe's highest-graded self-defence instructor, he has taught over 10,000 students, guided hundreds to Black Belt, and developed more than 50 instructors, establishing himself as a respected leader in discipline-based training.

Holding a BSc in Sport Science and a PGCE, and with over 5 years of experience as a professional lecturer, Dervish is known for making complex ideas simple, practical, and actionable. His academic background and hands-on teaching experience give him a rare ability to help students build clarity, confidence, and long-term consistency.

In 2007, he expanded his journey into property investing, applying the same structured, results-driven approach that defined his martial arts career. Over time, he built a strong, cash-flowing portfolio, paid off his mortgage in his early thirties, and created long-term financial security for his family. He continues to invest today, managing a portfolio designed for stability, freedom, and generational wealth.

Passionate about empowering others, Dervish blends Black Belt mindset, strategy, and systems to help people achieve real change. These principles run through his teaching, his mentorship, and now this book.

He is also the author of **'How To Build a Highly Profitable Martial Arts School'** and the founder of the **Black Belt Property Academy**, where he helps aspiring investors develop the discipline, knowledge, and confidence to succeed in property and beyond.

Dervish lives with his family, continuing to write, mentor, invest, and inspire the next generation of purpose-driven achievers.

Having mentored thousands to **Black Belt level, Dervish** and the **Black Belt Property Academy** apply the same discipline, structure, and standards to property investors.

Start Your Journey With The Black Belt Property Accelerator

This book was written to give you clarity.
Not hype.
Not shortcuts.

But reading and doing are not the same.
If you want to move from understanding property investing to applying it with discipline, the next step is structure and guidance.

The **Black Belt Property Accelerator** exists to install the foundations properly; deal analysis, decision-making, and investor discipline.

Learn more here:
DervishDervish.com

You don't need more information.
You need the right structure and the discipline to apply it.

Dervish Dervish
Founder, Black Belt Property Academy
6th Degree Black Belt | Author | BSc | PGCE

www.ingramcontent.com/pod-product-compliance
Lightning Source LLC
LaVergne TN
LVHW091523200926
848483LV00002B/290